RICHARD THE LIONHEART

Crusader King of England

TOM STREISSGUTH

Enslow Publishers, Inc.
40 Industrial Road
Box 398
Berkeley Heights, NJ 07922
USA
http://www.enslow.com

Library of Congress Cataloging-in-Publication Data:

Streissguth, Thomas, 1958-
    Richard the Lionheart : crusader king of England / Tom Streissguth.
        p. cm. — (Rulers of the Middle Ages)
    Includes bibliographical references and index.
    ISBN-13: 978-0-7660-2714-5
    ISBN-10: 0-7660-2714-7
    1. Richard I, King of England, 1157–1199—Juvenile literature. 2. Great Britain—
    History—Richard I, 1189–1199—Juvenile literature. 3. Great Britain—Kings and rulers—
    Biography—Juvenile literature. 4. Crusades—Third, 1189–1192—Juvenile literature.
    I. Title.
    DA207.S77 2006
    942.03'2092—dc22
    [B]

                                                        2006019229

Printed in the United States of America

10 9 8 7 6 5 4 3 2 1

To Our Readers:
We have done our best to make sure all Internet addresses in this book were active and appropriate
when we went to press. However, the author and the publisher have no control over and assume
no liability for the material available on those Internet sites or on other Web sites they may link
to. Any comments or suggestions can be sent by e-mail to comments@enslow.com or to the
address on the back cover.

Illustration Credits: AY Arktos, Wikipedia.org, p. 142; Enslow Publishers, Inc., pp. 18, 84; Eon
Images, p. 92; The Granger Collection, New York, pp. 16, 60, 75; Illustrated by Michael
Grimsdale/Saudi Aramco World/PADIA, p. 89; istockphoto.com/glubsch, p. 124; © 2006
Jupiterimages Corporation, pp. 30, 70, 79; Mary Evans Picture Library/The Image Works,
p. 139; Original Painting by Corey Wolfe, pp. 9, 57; Paul Cowan, Shutterstock, p. 4.

Illustration Used in Design: Reproduced from *Full-Color Picture Sourcebook of Historic
Ornament*, published by Dover Publications, Inc.

Cover Illustration: Original Painting by Corey Wolfe.

CONTENTS

This statue of Richard I stands outside the Parliament building in London, England.

INTRODUCTION

THE TIME WAS THE TWELFTH CENTURY A.D.
Europe was divided into kingdoms, duchies, and counties,
all ruled by noble families. The nobles were absolute
masters of their domain. They often fought with one
another over their titles, power, and land. The feudal
system made every man the vassal, or servant, of another.

It was a time of constant war and violence. Armored
knights fought on horseback. They skillfully used heavy
iron swords and long, sharp lances. They fought in small
groups or singly. When they were not fighting wars, they
took part in tournaments. Even these mock battles resulted
in many bloody deaths.

Centuries before, Christian missionaries had brought
their faith to northern Europe. France, England, Germany,
and other regions were now Christian. But Palestine, the
land where Jesus preached, had become a battleground.

The Byzantine Empire ruled Palestine until Muslims
arrived in the seventh century. The Muslim armies
conquered Palestine. They raised an important shrine, the
Dome of the Rock, in the city of Jerusalem. For Christians,
Jews, and Muslims, Jerusalem was a holy city. The land
surrounding it was the Holy Land.

In the year 1095, the pope of the Christian church
summoned Europe's knights and soldiers to fight the
"Turks," or Muslims. During this First Crusade,
Christians fought against Muslims for control of the Holy

Land. A Christian army conquered Jerusalem. The victors massacred the city's people. The Christians built fortresses to protect their conquests.

The Muslims fought back. The struggle continued for generations. In the late twelfth century, a skilled Muslim general named Saladin rose to power. He defeated the Christian armies and took back Jerusalem for Islam.

THE THIRD CRUSADE

On June 7, 1191, onlookers spotted a huge fleet of sailing ships from the shores of Palestine. There were hundreds of vessels, large and small. The ships were flying the banners of Richard I. He was the king of England and the ruler of the rich and powerful Angevin empire.

The onlookers knew well who Richard was. They said this king had never lost a battle. He was a master of siege warfare. No castle or fortified city had been able to resist his armies. Richard was now leading the Third Crusade to Jerusalem. He was the great hope of the Christian crusaders in the Holy Land.

Near the harbor of Acre, the king's fleet came across a Muslim supply ship. The ship was on its way to Acre. Its Muslim crew meant to reinforce the city. The city had been under siege by the Christians for three years.

To deceive the Christians, the Muslim ship was flying the flag of France. The Muslim commander had also ordered that several pigs be set free on the decks of his ship. Everyone knew that Muslims did not keep pigs or eat pork. The Muslims believed the Europeans would be fooled into believing the ship was European. The English king would allow it to pass.

Richard was expecting a trick. He was an experienced war veteran. He knew that a clever general will always seek to deceive a more powerful army, rather than fight. One of his crew spoke up to the king. "Sire," he said, "have mc slain or hanged, an [if] this ship be not a Turkish ship."[1]

Richard hailed the enemy ship. He flew signal flags and called out, asking it to stop. He sent a small boat into the water to approach the other ship. The captain of the other ship did not obey him. Instead, the ship's crew fired arrows at the small boat.

The Muslim admiral had several hundred soldiers on board.[2] The soldiers stoutly defended themselves, and the fight dragged on. Neither side won a victory, and neither side surrendered. Seeing the stalemate, Richard grew impatient.

The king of England would not be stopped by a single enemy ship before stepping ashore in the Holy Land. He ordered his ship's crew into the water. They swam under the Muslim ship and lashed its rudder with ropes. This prevented the Muslim ship from steering.

Under the press of the wind, the ship began going helplessly in circles. Richard then ordered his ship to ram the enemy. His ship had armor on its prow. The heavy prow slammed into the enemy ship, piercing its hull.

Several more English boats approached the Muslim vessel. English soldiers leaped aboard and began fighting with the crew of the enemy ship.

The Muslim admiral, now at Richard's mercy, ordered his men to sink their ship. He did not want the weapons and other supplies falling into the hands of the English.

The Muslim crew knocked holes into the hull of their ship. Water rushed in, and the ship began to sink. As it plunged into the sea, several hundred men fell into the water. Under Richard's orders, the Christians killed all but a few dozen of them.[3] They took the survivors as hostages.

A KING OF WARRIORS

Richard I had been king of England for less than two years. But he took little interest in the affairs of England. His homeland was Aquitaine, in southern France. War was his true interest and his first love. He went eagerly to any place that offered him a battle.

War in the Middle Ages was a test of strength and personal courage. People expected a king to be skilled with arms and an expert rider. If he did not accept battle with his enemies, he would lose respect, and possibly his crown as well.

Noblemen watched and waited for any signs of weakness. They did not hesitate to rebel against a king when they saw their chance. They had armies of their own and knights at their command. They raised castle strongholds to defend their land. Royal armies were much too small to keep order throughout an entire kingdom.

It took a strong personality to rule any stretch of land. But Richard was perfectly matched to his role and his times. He was forceful and energetic. He was loyal to

Richard was known for his skillful war tactics and bravery in battle.

friends and merciless to enemies. He knew how to lead common soldiers and fire them with courage and enthusiasm. Men of many different nations followed him into battle.

Richard lived and died by the violence of his age. But he was more than a great warrior. He was a brilliant military and political strategist. He outmaneuvered enemy armies and outwitted his many rivals. In a family of ambitious and violent men, he rose to the top and stayed there.

In Palestine, Richard would finally meet his match in Saladin. He would face the hardest and most dangerous test of his life. This great combat would have lasting effects in Europe and Palestine. It would also make Richard's reputation as one of the finest military leaders in history.

THE ANGEVIN REALM

IN THE FIFTH CENTURY A.D., THE WESTERN Roman Empire fell. The powerful armies of Rome disappeared from northern Europe. Germanic tribes invaded the cities of Gaul (now the nation of France). Angles and Saxons from northern Germany overran the island of Britain.

These tribes had no written law, only customs. The people settled their feuds privately. They were loyal only to chieftains who had proved themselves in battle.

For centuries, Gaul was a chaotic and violent place. The Germanic tribes lived in small settlements, surrounded by walls of stone or wood. Very few people traveled the dangerous roads, where bands of robbers threatened them. There were no governments, no armies, and no police forces to maintain order.

The countryside was the scene of pitched battles between small warrior bands. Men fought on foot, while a few of their leaders rode horses into battle. The bands fought for control of strongholds. They built new strongholds on hilltops and near rivers. These natural features made places easier to defend.

In her book *A Short History of the Middle Ages*, Barbara Rosenwein describes what a traveler would see in the countryside of England:

> . . . fenced wooden farmsteads, each with a rectangular "hall" for eating and sleeping, a few outbuildings serving as sheds, and perhaps a sunken house, its floor below the level of the soil. . . . Fields were planted with barley (used to make a thick and nourishing beer) as well as oats, wheat, and rye. . . . There were many animals: sheep, goats, horses, cattle, pigs, and dogs.[1]

Some fortified places grew into small cities. The people raised houses, shops, and markets within the walls. At the center of the settlement was a tower, or keep. The keep was the tallest structure for miles around. It served the lord of the city as a headquarters. The city also used it as a prison. The lord of the city kept his valuables and gold in the keep.

A company of soldiers guarded the walls. Lookouts kept an eye on the countryside. When necessary, they came out to defend the surrounding fields. Raiders could appear at any moment. If they could not break through the walls, they might begin a siege.

Sieges were long and costly. Both sides suffered hunger, impatience, and fear. The enemy burned the surrounding land so it produced no food. They allowed no one to enter or leave. If the people of the city did not surrender, or fight

their way out, they starved. Sieges could last for weeks
or months.

THE ANGEVIN KINGDOM

After the fall of Rome, dozens of small kingdoms emerged
in France and England. The Anglo-Saxon kingdoms of
England often went to war. The French kings ruled a court
that moved from place to place. Their power base lay in
Paris and some surrounding territory. They had no
authority in Normandy, Anjou, or Aquitaine. These
territories were independent.

The leaders of the French domains raised powerful
armies to protect this independence. They allied with one
another through marriage. They arranged these marriages
when their children were very young. The boys and girls of
the ruling families served as useful tools in the quest for
power and land.

In the twelfth century, much of western France
belonged to the counts of Anjou. Their Angevin realm lay
on both sides of the Loire River. Anjou extended east to the
Touraine and south to Poitou and Aquitaine. To the north
of the Angevin realm was the duchy of Normandy.

The cities of France earned money through trade. A
class of merchants formed a growing middle class. They
traveled the roads, selling their wares. Artisans earned
money by their skill as carpenters or masons. They helped
to raise large castles in the countryside. In the cities, the
people built towering cathedrals.

The peasants, most with no land of their own, worked the fields as serfs. They were the property of landowning aristocrats. Most peasants lived in poverty. Hard work, disease, and violence often cut short their lives.

War and sieges were still common in this world. The nobles who owned cities and estates fought constantly with one another. Small bands of heavily armed knights and mercenaries (men who fought only for pay) roamed across the land. They attacked rivals by burning their villages and killing the people.

THE PLANTAGENET DYNASTY

In 1128, an important wedding took place. Geoffrey Plantagenet, the heir to the county of Anjou, married Matilda. She was the daughter of Henry I, the king of England and duke of Normandy. A few years later, Henry I died.

Henry had favored a cousin, Stephen of Blois, as his successor. But Matilda and Geoffrey also had a claim to the crown. When Stephen arrived in England, the English barons supported him as their new ruler. Stephen's son, Eustace, became the heir to the throne. Geoffrey fought back. In the 1140s, he conquered Normandy and wrested it from Stephen.

Geoffrey remained in Anjou. In 1151, before he could invade England and claim Matilda's inheritance, he died. By his will, he passed Anjou to his son Henry. In the next year, the young Henry Plantagenet married Eleanor. She

POPE URBAN CALLS FOR A CRUSADE

The Christian church was an important institution in medieval Europe. The church controlled many aspects of daily life. Priests and bishops had as much authority as nobles and kings, with whom ordinary people had little contact.

But since the time of Jesus Christ, a new religion had arisen in the Middle East. In the seventh century, the prophet Muhammad established Islam in Arabia. Muslim armies conquered the city of Jerusalem, holy to Jews, Christians, and Muslims alike.

European Christians dreamed of taking back Jerusalem from the Muslims. In 1095, Pope Urban II called for a crusade to do just that. The First Crusade took place soon afterward. Christian armies conquered Jerusalem and several other important cities in the Holy Land.

The struggle for the Holy Land did not end with this Christian victory. There would be several more Crusades, and many more battles. Richard Plantagenet and many others grew up with the dream of fighting Muslims in the Holy Land. After he became the king of England, he would have his chance.

was the heiress to the wealthy duchy of Aquitaine in southern France.

In January 1153, Henry sailed to England. There he rallied an army against King Stephen and his son, Eustace. By this time, Stephen had grown unpopular in England. His harsh rule turned the wealthy barons of the realm against him.

King Henry II arrives with his queen, Eleanor of Aquitaine, in Winchester, England on the day in December 1154 that he became king.

The armies of Henry and Stephen marched through southern England, skirmishing when they met. Then, in August 1153, Stephen of Blois suffered a heavy blow—the death of his son, Eustace. According to some histories, Eustace had choked to death on a plate of eels.

Stephen now had no heir for the throne of England. He agreed to recognize Henry Plantagenet as his heir. The barons of England paid homage to Henry as their future lord. In December 1154, Henry Plantagenet became Henry II, king of England. This event established the Plantagenet dynasty in England.

PLANTAGENET ENGLAND

At this time, England was a realm of wealthy landowners and poor farmers. Sheep raising was an important occupation.

The English sold their wool all over the continent of Europe. Silver mines supplied the king with money to pay armies and raise castles.

The peasants worked the land and paid rent to landowners. Because money was scarce, they paid with the crops they raised. Few of these peasants had land of their own. Very few of them could escape their station in life. They depended on the weather and a good growing season. If they had a bad crop, they starved.

Men could escape this life by joining the army as a foot soldier or archer. Some became highwaymen, robbing stray travelers of their money and sometimes their lives. Others went on a crusade, seeking glory and riches while fighting to recapture the Holy Land from the Muslims.

For the lord of the manor, life was very different. Many of those who owned land profited well from the crops and livestock raised by their peasants. To guard their domains, these nobles built castles in places difficult to attack.

Castles had wood or stone walls. At the base of the walls was a moat, a ditch sometimes filled with water from a nearby river. Battlements at the top of the wall allowed defenders to rain down arrows, stones, or hot oil on the enemy.

The possession of a castle allowed a noble to protect his territory. It also allowed him, if he liked, to defy the armies of the king. For this reason, the English kings took care to keep the nobles in check.

Henry sent loyal garrisons to defend his royal castles. These soldiers could be sent quickly to any trouble spots. His sheriffs, who ruled the English counties, also watched

ENGLAND AND
FRANCE, 1154

SCOTLAND

North Sea

Irish Sea

WALES ENGLAND

N
W E
S

English Channel

FLANDERS
•Bouvines

•Rouen

CHAMPAGNE

NORMANDY
Tinchebrai• •Falalso •Paris
BRITTANY
MAINE
Le Mans• Orleans

•Chinon
BURGUNDY
Poitiers•
POITOU

Atlantic Ocean

AQUITAINE AUVERGNE

TOULOUSE

Land of English Kings
Land of French Kings
Independent French Land

During the reign of Henry II, the English ruled much of the
land in France.

out for any rebellion. Loyal judges, whom Henry appointed, brought any troublemakers into court and punished them severely.

THE COURT OF HENRY II

Henry II held authority over the largest and wealthiest state in Europe, stretching from northern England to western France and the Pyrenees Mountains. His queen, Eleanor, reigned over a court in Poitiers, the capital of Aquitaine. Both king and queen had incredible energy, riding constantly throughout their huge domain. The king put down revolts and made his presence known to lords and peasants alike.

In the words of historian Amy Kelly: "Henry was wont to appear, here, there, and everywhere, when he was least expected. Even his own clerks bringing him news of importance could not find him or catch up with him."[2]

Henry's court included several hundred people. It was a mobile court, which moved from one town to the next. Henry spent little time in the royal castles, in London or on the continent.

Supporting this community was a heavy burden. According to Kelly:

> "The royal household [was] equipped with chapel, bed furnishings, kitchen utensils, plate, treasure, garments, vestments, documents . . . The abbots of monasteries where the king was privileged to billet his horses and his men would rather have welcomed a swarm of locusts than the royal company."[3]

The Angevin empire became the strongest rival to the king of France, Louis VII. King Louis was a member of the Capetian dynasty. The Capetian kings controlled Paris and the lands bordering Normandy and Anjou. Louis was an enemy of Henry II. Eleanor of Aquitaine had once been his wife. But Eleanor had no sons by Louis. Her marriage to Henry ended any claims Louis had to Aquitaine.

But Henry did not want war with Louis. He had trouble enough controlling his own lands and nobles. Henry agreed to meet the French king in February 1156. In a formal ceremony, Henry paid homage to Louis. By this medieval custom, one man agrees to serve another as his vassal. He vows to remain loyal and to fight for his overlord when called upon. The lord, in turn, vows to protect his vassal.

By paying homage, Henry agreed to be the vassal of Louis in Normandy, Anjou, and Aquitaine. He recognized the French king's authority in those lands. This was the first time a king of England would ever pay homage to a king of France. But instead of bringing peace, it would lead to centuries of warfare between the two nations.

THE BIRTH OF A PRINCE

On September 8, 1157, Eleanor gave birth to a son at the palace of Beaumont, in the English city of Oxford. This was her third son, and he was named Richard. With Henry, she had already had two sons. Henry had given her firstborn, William, the title of count of Poitiers. But William had died in 1156. The parents gave their second son the name of Henry. His nickname would be Young Henry, or the Young King.

Although Richard was born in England, he grew up in France. He spent most of his youth at his mother's court in Poitiers. He became the favorite son of his mother.

Royal tutors schooled Richard Plantagenet. He learned to compose music and write Latin (the ancient language of Rome). He spoke French and Provençal, the language of southern France.

Richard also learned the arts of riding, hunting, and fighting. He grew skilled with a sword, mace, and shield, the weapons of a medieval warrior. As part of his training, he also took part in tournaments.

Tournaments were the grand sporting events of the Middle Ages. In these contests, several knights joined together as a company to fight on horseback with swords and lances.

The tournament battles ranged over hills and forests. They could last an entire day. The contestants risked injury and death in contests of strength and fighting skill. By custom, the victorious team won the armor and horses of the losers.

Tournaments could also include single combat, also known as jousting. This dangerous game of strength and bravery took place before a crowd of spectators. Two knights in armor rode their best horses. They began at the two ends of a long field. The horses galloped toward the center. Each knight held out his lance, seeking to strike the other and throw him off his horse.

Tournaments improved the fighting ability of those who took part. At a young age, Richard was meeting opponents in these contests. He was a strong and skilled combatant. He also was protected by his rank. No knight would dare to bring harm to the heir of Henry II.

Richard also learned the manners and customs of his father's court. By the code of chivalry, every man owed loyalty to a superior. His lands belonged to him only through the grace of a noble or king. He had to act with humility to his lord, with mercy to opponents, and with good manners toward women.

In the royal household lived the Plantagenet family as well as aristocrats, officials, knights, servants, and entertainers. In the evenings, the court gathered for meals and conversation. In this setting, it was important for a young prince to speak well. He had to hold himself with pride and dignity. He also had to display the vital quality of courtesy.

To be courteous was to act with proper manners, as a respected member of a noble court. The rough and often brutal manners of the past were no longer in style. Good style and politeness at the dinner table marked a noble man or woman. According to one account:

> Various "Bokes of Curtesye" laid out the table manners expected of a polite dinner guest. A gentleman was permitted to pick out tasty morsels with his fingers and offer them to his companion, but he was discouraged from buttering bread with his thumb, poking his finger into eggs, or wiping his teeth on the tablecloth.[4]

Richard's mother, Eleanor, had played an important role in this change of manners. She had brought skilled poets, troubadours (singers), and writers to her court in Poitiers, the capital of Aquitaine.

The love poetry and songs these courtiers wrote were all the rage in Europe in the twelfth century. Eleanor's palace in Poitiers was the capital of a new style in art and manners. A tradition of courtly love spread from Poitiers to the rest of Europe.

A TRAVELING KING

While Richard was growing up, Henry traveled through his domains. He lived in the households of the rich. He also stayed in rough hostels and inns. If night came, and he was still on the road, he slept in the open.

Henry never stopped riding. It was important for the subjects of Henry II to see their king. His visits helped their respect for his authority. In the words of historian James Brundage:

> "The king . . . bristled with an almost superhuman energy. Physically strong, stocky of build, deep-chested, red-haired, Henry possessed a robust constitution. He was always on the move and perennially scheming to enlarge his power and his lands."[5]

A strong-minded, energetic king had the best chance to keep the loyalty of the people he ruled. If he were lazy or weak, he would soon have a rebellion on his hands. Ambitious nobles would raid his domains and claim territory for themselves. A rival king would make war on him. A war was always raging somewhere in medieval Europe.

Henry's travel throughout his realm did not prevent defiance on the part of his own vassals. In 1168, two powerful nobles of Aquitaine, the count of Angouleme and Geoffrey de Lusignan, allied against Henry. In retaliation, Henry raided the castle of the Lusignan family. He burned the surrounding countryside, the Lusignan domains.

Henry won the victory, but he still needed strong allies. In March, he signed a treaty with Louis, the king of France. Louis recognized Richard as the heir to Aquitaine. It also engaged Richard to marry Alais, the daughter of the French king.

Richard was only ten years old. In his day, parents often engaged their children long before the children could marry. Sons and daughters had no say in the matter. Marriage alliances were a useful tool for kings and nobles who sought to avoid war.

The agreement of March 1168 did not stop the fighting. The next January, after several more months of violence and raiding, Henry and Louis again made peace. They signed the Treaty of Montmirail. The young Richard, now eleven years old, did homage to Louis as his vassal in Aquitaine. The kings again agreed to have Richard marry Alais.

With no interference from Louis, Henry turned against the rebels of Aquitaine. He attacked with a vengeance, burning castles and imprisoning his enemies. By 1172, southern France was firmly under Henry's control again.

THE DUKE OF AQUITAINE

In that year, Richard made an important journey to Poitiers. He sat on a throne in the Abbey of Saint Hilary. He received a sacred banner, the symbol of his lordship over Aquitaine.

In another ceremony at Limoges, he was given the ring of Saint Valerie, the patron saint of the duchy. He was now the duke of Aquitaine—but still the subject of his father, Henry II.

Richard's days of schooling and training had ended. He was now the lord of a vast territory, covering what is now southwestern France. Although he was only fourteen years old, it was now his task to keep the duchy peaceful and obedient to him.

The young duke had already gained a reputation as a skilled and energetic fighter, who was also able to write poetry and music in several languages. One chronicler described him as follows: "He was tall of stature, graceful in figure; his hair between red and auburn, his limbs were straight and flexible; his arms rather long, and not to be matched for wielding the sword or for striking with it, and his long legs suited the rest of his frame."[6]

But Richard also had his flaws. He was an impatient man who rarely thought about the consequences of his actions. He cared little for his father and would often be disloyal to him. He often acted out of selfishness and greed.

Richard had a difficult task in ruling Aquitaine. There were hundreds of wealthy estates within the borders of the duchy. There were several powerful nobles with lands of their own. They kept large companies of knights and mercenaries who would fight for the highest pay.

These nobles of Aquitaine had little respect for a fourteen-year-old boy, no matter who his father was. Richard soon found that Aquitaine would not gently accept his rule. He would have to fight to claim his own inheritance.

THE SONS OF HENRY REBEL

In the meantime, Young Henry, Richard's elder brother, was growing frustrated and angry. His own inheritance was to be Anjou and Normandy. He would also be the king of England. But his father would still not allow Henry control of these rich territories. The rents and tribute from these lands went into Henry II's treasury, not that of his son.

The king did not trust anyone, even his own children. He granted titles to them but denied them real authority. He did not share the income of the Angevin realm with them or anyone else.

Eleanor supported her sons in this dispute. She plotted with Young Henry and Richard, as well as her younger son, Geoffrey, to make war on the king. She wanted Aquitaine, her homeland, to remain under Richard's firm control.

To help their cause, the three brothers went to Paris to meet with King Louis. They allied with the French king and plotted with him against their father. In 1173, a civil war erupted.

Several of Henry's vassals joined the rebellion. These included the Lusignan family, Count William of Angouleme, and Geoffrey de Rancon. He was the lord of Taillebourg, a castle with walls so high and thick it was said no army could conquer it.

In the summer of 1173, Richard and his brothers invaded Normandy. They joined an army led by Philip, the count of Flanders. But when Philip's brother was killed in the fighting, the count abandoned the fight.

Without the help of the count of Flanders, the rebellion had little chance to succeed. The armies of Henry II were too strong. The sons of Henry agreed to meet their father for peace talks. They met at the fortress of Gisors, on the border between Normandy and France.

Henry offered to share the money earned from his domains with his sons. But he would not give up his authority over the Angevin lands. His sons refused the offer.

Late that year, Eleanor, while traveling in disguise, was captured by men loyal to Henry II. The king had her brought to England. He kept her prisoner in a country mansion. When he heard this news, Richard grew angry. He vowed to defeat his father and rescue his mother.

He formed an army and invaded Poitou, the territory lying between Anjou and Aquitaine. He set up his headquarters in the city of Saintes. He gathered knights and archers and waited for an opportunity to attack the main army of Henry, in the city of Poitiers.

Henry proved too quick and smart for his sixteen-year-old son. He quickly attacked Saintes, taking Richard completely by surprise. As Henry's knights galloped through the city streets, Richard fled the city in a small company of loyal men. Richard's company soon reached the stronghold of Taillebourg.

Richard knew he could hold out for months in Taillebourg. Henry, in the meantime, overran Aquitaine. He defeated the nobles who had joined the rebellion. In September 1174, Henry and Louis finally called a truce. Geoffrey saw no advantage in pressing the fight without the French king's help. He had his army retreat to Brittany.

Seeing that further fighting was useless, Richard surrendered to his father. He threw himself to the ground before the king and asked Henry to forgive him.

Henry showed mercy to his rebellious son. At the town of Montlouis, Henry and Richard made their peace. Richard was allowed to share the money earned from Aquitaine. Henry also gave him two castles for his court and his army. The nobles who had joined him were allowed to return to their domains.

Henry then ordered Richard to besiege castles in Aquitaine that had been raised by the rebel leaders. Richard was to attack these castles and demand their surrender. If the defenders resisted, he was to burn the strongholds to the ground.

Henry forgave his son because he needed Richard to rule Aquitaine. But the rebellion made Henry suspicious and mistrustful.

Eleanor fared much worse than Richard. She would remain Henry's prisoner. Mistrusting her, the king had her closely guarded in a castle in England.

THE SIEGE OF TAILLEBOURG

THE TREATY OF MONTLOUIS ENDED THE WAR between Henry II and his sons. Richard and Henry the Younger called home their troops. The king allowed Richard to keep two castles in Aquitaine. Richard also had the right to keep half of the income of this domain.

Both sides freed the prisoners they held for ransom. One prisoner did not enjoy her freedom: Eleanor of Aquitaine. King Henry kept Richard's mother under close guard. She could move from one castle to the next in England. But she could not return to the Poitevin. Henry did not let her travel anywhere on her own. The king's spies read all of her messages and followed her every movement.

Henry also was very suspicious of Richard. He saw this son as the most capable warrior of all his sons. He knew Richard could lead men and win campaigns. Richard also had a wealthy domain of his own—Aquitaine. He could use this duchy to gather allies and raise armies for war.

LAMENT FOR ELEANOR

The news of Eleanor of Aquitaine's captivity spread throughout Europe. She had inspired a new style in manners and art at her court in Poitiers. Now she was a prisoner of her own husband, King Henry II, in England.

Poets and troubadours in Europe wrote sad songs about the famous prisoner. The chronicler Richard le Poitevin wrote the following lament:

Daughter of Aquitaine, fair, fruitful vine! Tell me, Eagle with two heads, tell me: where were you when your eaglets, flying from their nest, dared to raise their talons against the King of the North Wind? It was you, we learned, who urged them to rise against their father. That is why you have been ravished from your own country and carried away to a strange land.[1]

To check Richard's ambitions, Henry gave more power to his younger son, John. He granted John castles and land. He also named John as the ruler of Ireland. He arranged John's marriage to Isabelle of Gloucester. She was the daughter of the earl of Gloucester, the richest earldom in England.

BREAKING THE MARRIAGE CONTRACT

Henry had one more way of cutting Richard down to size. He delayed the wedding of Richard and Alais, the daughter of King Louis of France. This action angered both Richard and Louis. But Henry had good reason to block the marriage.

Henry did not want to see Richard ally himself with the king of France. He knew that with the French army and king beside him, Richard would be unstoppable. A new rebellion would endanger Henry's own authority in Normandy and Anjou. Henry believed Richard might even invade England.

To carry out his plan, Henry took Alais as his own mistress. He kept her hidden away in his court and did not allow her to leave. Henry knew that Richard was full of pride. Richard would reject Alais as a wife, if he knew that she had been his father's lover.

These actions also angered Philip, the half-brother of Alais and the future king of France. Philip knew the marriage of Alais to Richard would strengthen the claim of France on Angevin lands and property. In his book *The Shade of Swords*, the modern Islamic historian Muhammad J. Akbar offers this viewpoint:

> In 1161, Philip's beautiful half-sister Alais was promised to Richard . . . Alais was consequently sent to the court to learn English manners, such as they were, and be ready for Richard. . . . Philip insisted that Richard should honour the pledge to marry a woman who was now his father's mistress as he [Philip] wanted the castle in Gisors that had been promised as part of the marriage settlement.[2]

SKILLED IN WAR AND SIEGES

Henry still had trouble with the nobles of Aquitaine. In 1175, under Henry's orders, Richard campaigned in the duchy. He attacked and destroyed several castles under the control of rebel nobles. He skirmished with roaming bands of looters and mercenaries. He hired some of these mercenaries to fight with his own company.

Richard grew skilled in the art of siege warfare. He collected rams, catapults, and other artillery weapons. He used these powerful weapons against the stone walls of enemy strongholds. He also learned to negotiate. The lords of some castles accepted his offers of peace. If they defied his terms, Richard starved them out with a long siege.

A few would not surrender. With large stores of food, they could hold out for months. With the protection of the walls, defenders could keep a much larger enemy at bay for weeks or months. In the meantime, Richard's own army struggled to survive.

When faced with a long siege, Richard ordered an assault. His men raised stout ladders against the walls and climbed into the battlements. They fought hand to hand, with swords and daggers. Their goal was the castle keep. By capturing the keep, they could seize weapons and free prisoners.

Richard learned to be very careful about ordering a direct assault. He never ordered one unless he had a strong advantage in numbers. If a victory seemed too difficult, he withdrew his troops. It was most important to preserve scarce fighting men.

SIEGE WARFARE

Richard was unable to subdue all of the enemies of the Plantagenets. In early 1176, Viscount Aimar of Limoges revolted against Angevin control. Aimar enlisted several other powerful nobles as allies.

At every opportunity, the rebels attacked the territories under Plantagenet control. Their object was to destroy crops, homes, shops, and villages. By doing this, they prevented people from paying taxes and rent to the Plantagenet rulers.

Henry asked his sons Richard and Henry the Younger to subdue this new rebellion in the spring of 1176. He provided the brothers with large sums of gold and silver. The brothers used the money to hire mercenaries. They equipped their men with horses and good weapons.

Richard ordered a march into Aimar's territory near the city of Limoges. He quickly captured Aixe, an important castle. In June, he began a siege of Limoges itself. Within a few days, the city surrendered, although Aimar escaped. The Plantagenet armies next attacked the castle of Chateauneuf, capturing it in two weeks.

Unhappy that his brother was winning all the glory and honors, Henry the Younger left the campaign. As the oldest brother, Henry believed he should have authority over Richard. But the common soldiers followed Richard, not Henry. They didn't believe Henry to be a good military leader.

The rebel leaders saw that trouble was again brewing in the Plantagenet family. They decided to fight on, hoping for complete independence. They gathered in the city of Angouleme. They brought weapons, knights, and several thousand archers, infantry, and mercenaries. They fortified the city and took shelter within its walls.

Richard pressed on, laying siege to Angouleme. He organized an assault with his artillery. Huge stones crashed into the walls. Richard's archers kept up a constant rain of arrows into the streets of Angouleme. In just six days, the city surrendered.

Richard took Count William of Angouleme and Viscount Aimar of Limoges as prisoners. In September, he sent them to England to beg for mercy from King Henry.

CLEARING THE ROAD TO SPAIN

Richard did not stop at Angouleme. He gathered more mercenaries in the fall of 1176. His goal was to clear the road leading from Aquitaine to Spain. Every year, Christian pilgrims traveled this road to the shrine of Santiago de Compostella in northern Spain. Some rode horseback, and some walked. A few pilgrims crawled on their hands and knees.

Since the rebellion began, the road had become a war zone. It had come under the control of the Aquitaine rebels. They defied Duke Richard by robbing pilgrims and blocking the way. Many pilgrims and ordinary travelers died at their hands.

In January 1177, Richard's troops swept down the road. Richard captured castles at Dax, Bayonne, and Cize on the border of Spain. His reputation as a general was quickly growing. Most defenders surrendered when his army arrived at their walls.

Richard made a simple demand of all the princes and landowners of these parts. They must allow free passage to pilgrims on their way to Santiago de Compostella. They must not attack or hinder these pilgrims in any way. Terrified of Richard's mercenaries and his skill at siege warfare, the lords of southern Aquitaine agreed.

This campaign rewarded Richard with military glory. He also earned religious merit. It was the duty of every medieval prince to fight for the church, when necessary. Such service gave a prince high standing in the eyes of God. It cleansed away the sins of pride and greed.

The men of the church encouraged princes and kings to defend Christianity. They often preached against the Muslims, who controlled Palestine, the biblical Holy Land. They spoke of the Crusades against the Muslims, which began in 1095.

Their words fired Richard with enthusiasm. To pursue a glorious Christian crusade was the mark of a great warrior. He would journey to the other end of the Mediterranean Sea to fight for Palestine and the city of Jerusalem.

THE TWO KINGS MEET

The end of the rebellion in Aquitaine did not settle matters between Henry II and Louis, the king of France. Years before, the two men had agreed to the marriage of Richard Plantagenet and Princess Alais, the daughter of Louis. But now, Henry delayed the planned wedding. His actions made Louis angry and vengeful.

In September 1177, Louis and Henry met to hammer out their differences. At the town of Nonancourt, in Normandy, they made another agreement. They would keep the peace between them. Henry agreed to have Richard married to Alais. The two kings also agreed to go on a crusade together to the Holy Land.

For the next year, Richard remained in Aquitaine. He held court in the town of Saintes, on the Charente River. He kept watch on the property of the Angevins. As his father did, he rode from town to town to appear before the people. His reputation as a military leader was growing. Many believed him to be the best general in Europe. He had never suffered defeat. In this territory few had the will to challenge his mastery.

Still, opposition to the Angevins ran high among the nobles of Angouleme. The defeat of Count William of Angouleme had been a bitter blow to Vulgrin, William's son and heir. Vulgrin had ambitions to become the master of Angouleme and the region surrounding the city. While Richard held court at Saintes, Vulgrin made an alliance with Geoffrey de Rancon.

The two men held powerful castles at Pons and Taillebourg. By late 1178, they were openly defiant of Richard Plantagenet. They refused to come to Saintes to do homage to the duke. This was a direct challenge to Richard's authority.

Richard set out with his forces on the road to Pons. Geoffrey knew Richard's reputation as a skilled besieger of castles. He prepared his defenses and collected a good supply of food.

The siege of Pons dragged on for several months, into the spring of 1179. Finally, Richard decided to leave a small company of men at Pons. He pressed on with his main force to the north. He quickly captured the castle of Richemont and several others under Geoffrey's control. In May 1179, he reached the thick stone walls of Taillebourg.

AT THE STRONGHOLD OF TAILLEBOURG

The fortress of Taillebourg rose high on a steep rock overlooking the Charente River. It was visible for several miles around. The fortress was protected by natural cliffs and two circuits of walls. At the base of the walls lay a small village. The people could take shelter, if necessary, within the castle. They said that Taillebourg had never fallen to a siege.

Richard himself had taken shelter here in 1174, while pursued by the knights of his father, King Henry II. Now he was the besieger. He felt confident of final victory. He brought massive catapults and a small army to the base of the cliffs.

Richard carefully planned his assault on Taillebourg. He used psychology as well as artillery. He brought up his siege weapons and bombarded the walls at their weakest point. He ordered his men to pillage the town lying at the base of the walls. His soldiers burned homes and destroyed crops. They killed everyone they captured, in plain sight of the castle defenders.

Richard also placed his own camp close to the castle entrance. He made sure the enemy could see him. He walked among his men, giving orders and encouragement. He dared and hoped the defenders would try a counterattack.

The plan worked. When the castle garrison came out to fight, Richard ordered his men to rush the gates. The soldiers of the garrison fell back before the duke. He personally led his men into the battle. They saw him fighting with great spirit and skill.

The enemy saw the fierce loyalty of Richard's men. They knew these spirited troops would fight to the last. They also feared the pitiless treatment of their town, if they held out for very long. Very quickly, they surrendered. Taillebourg fell to the Angevins and the revolt of Geoffrey de Rancon came to a violent end.

In Richard Plantagenet's time, the siege of an ordinary castle might take weeks or even months. Many sieges failed completely. But Richard's defeat of Taillebourg, one of the strongest fortresses in all of France, had taken only three days.

The victory at Taillebourg was Richard's most famous success in battle. It made his reputation throughout Europe as a skilled commander. The defeat of the Aquitaine rebels also made the Plantagenet dynasty supreme in western France. Henry II and his sons now ruled from Normandy to the borders of Spain.

REBELLIONS IN THE ANGEVIN REALM

IN AUGUST 1179, KING LOUIS SUFFERED A STROKE.
The stroke paralyzed him and left him unable to rule. He
turned over the throne of France to Philip, his son by his
third wife, Adele. In November, during a grand ceremony at
the cathedral of Rheims, Philip was crowned King Philip II
of France.

Philip was only fifteen years old. By custom, a regent
ruled on behalf of a boy who held the title of king (France
never had a queen). But Philip had the strength and ability
to rule on his own.

Philip had great ambitions for France. He wanted to
unite all of its duchies, counties, and other domains. The
king of France, in his opinion, should rule Normandy,
Anjou, and Aquitaine. France would become a great empire.
This realm and its nobles would obey the French king.

Henry II and the Angevin empire stood in the way. For the time being, Philip kept the peace with Henry. In June 1180, the two kings met at Gisors, where they vowed to remain allies. In September 1180, Louis of France died.

These events did not end feuding within the Plantagenet dynasty. Another clash occurred in 1182. This feud arose from the jealousy of Young Henry, Richard Plantagenet's brother.

The achievements of Richard had made Young Henry, the oldest brother, envious. He sought a way to seize his rightful authority. He convinced his father, Henry II, to demand that Richard pay homage. Young Henry wanted Richard to formally pay his respects.

Henry II feared that the Angevin empire would break up if Richard did not agree. He believed Young Henry had right on his side, this time. He commanded Richard to pay homage to his elder brother.

But Richard refused to submit to anybody. He believed that Aquitaine belonged to him alone. He was the ruler, the duke of Aquitaine. He was nobody's vassal, and Young Henry had no say in his duchy.

To put Richard in his place, Henry II encouraged his eldest son to help the rebels in Aquitaine. Young Henry enthusiastically agreed. He was eager to make war on Richard. He asked his brother Geoffrey to help him. Geoffrey felt no loyalty to Richard. His main interest in life was to wrest more land and power from his rivals.

Geoffrey gathered an army in Brittany and joined Young Henry. The brothers found many allies in Aquitaine. Richard was ruling the duchy with an iron hand. He punished those he mistrusted by seizing their property and burning their lands. But Richard was still the best military leader in Europe.

Richard struck with lightning speed. He drove his men two days and nights to the town of Gorre. He attacked a group of mercenaries who were pillaging a church. His men killed several of the enemy and took many prisoners.

Richard made an example of these men. He had some thrown into a river and drowned. Others he had executed by having their throats cut. The rest had their eyes put out. Blinded, they were sure never to raise arms against Richard again.

Humiliated and frustrated by this defeat, Young Henry then went on a rampage. He attacked the castles and lands of his father as well as those of Richard. The struggle within the Plantagenet family turned into a civil war. Armies crisscrossed the countryside. They besieged castles and destroyed many villages.

The Angevin domains of France fell into chaos. King Philip helped one side, then the other. His goal was to weaken the Angevin realm and seize its territory. In the Plantagenet quarrel he saw a great opportunity for France.

THE YOUNG KING REBELS

Henry II saw that the clash among his sons was getting out of hand. He rode to Limoges, the rebel headquarters. He meant to talk with his son Henry and make peace within the family. He also sent messengers to Richard. He asked Richard to come to Limoges and join the truce.

Henry's company arrived in the Limousin region, the headquarters of the Aquitaine rebellion. He approached the castle of Limoges. Here Count Aimar commanded his knights and infantry. Henry had joined his forces with those of the rebellious count.

Richard had agreed to come to Limoges. From the battlements, Count Aimar and the rebels kept a wary eye on the duke. But Richard had not come to fight. He joined his father in the open field at the base of the castle walls.

Young Henry sent out messengers, asking his father and brother to negotiate a truce with Aimar and the rebels. Henry agreed, but as he stood before the walls of a castle, an arrow shot from the top of the wall struck the king. Protected by a suit of chain mail, King Henry suffered only a minor wound.

That evening, Young Henry came out from the castle to apologize for the stray arrow. The shot was an accident, and he meant his father no harm. But King Henry felt insulted by his son's manner and by the attack on his person, which he believed to be no accident. He angrily sent his son away from the camp.

The next day, the same thing happened. As Henry was riding before the castle, another archer fired an arrow in his direction. The arrow struck the king's horse in the neck. The horse reared up in fright, nearly throwing the king to the ground.

Henry the Younger came out again to apologize. To show his regret, he offered his own horse and weapons to his father.

The two Henrys sat down together to hammer out their differences. Henry angrily criticized his eldest son. He believed Young Henry unfit to rule the Angevin empire. A king needed to be a diplomat as well as a warrior. In the elder man's opinion, Young Henry was neither.

AN ENEMY OF THE PEOPLE

For several days, the Plantagenets kept the peace at Limoges. In the meantime, the rebels left the castle to burn homes and loot the surrounding countryside. At their head was Geoffrey of Brittany, the younger brother of Henry and Richard.

Geoffrey cared nothing for settling differences with anybody. He didn't care about the Plantagenet dynasty or the Angevin empire. He was greedy, sly, and violent.

Geoffrey's men went on a rampage that lasted for weeks. They attacked churches and monasteries and looted the treasuries of these holy places. They captured dozens of monks and priests and held them prisoner. They demanded ransom from the church.

Meanwhile, at Limoges, Young Henry grew frustrated by his father's angry lectures, which seemed to have no end. Young Henry left Limoges. He intended to make war on his brother and his father. He wandered through the Limousin region, taking refuge in castles and monasteries. He led his loyal knights and men on raids to gather money and horses.

Instead of a respected prince, Young Henry became an enemy of the people. Far and wide, he was seen as a greedy, worthless, and dangerous son. One writer, Peter of Blois, sent the young king a letter to demand an explanation for his actions:

> You make yourself an enemy of God and Justice and a transgressor of all laws if you do not obey your father to whom you owe all that you are . . . For who provides for your material existence? Your father. Who educated you? Your father. Who bred you to arms? Your father. Who put himself aside to make you king? Your father. Who labored in every way that you might possess all things in peace? Your father. . . . Where is your filial affection? Where is your reverence? Where is the law of nature? Where [is] your fear of God?[1]

THE DEATH OF AN HEIR

Young Henry's actions came out of jealousy of his younger brother Richard. He also felt slighted by his father's decisions. His father had given Richard rich territories in Poitou and Aquitaine. Richard commanded a powerful force of loyal knights and foot soldiers. He had won glory and honor at Taillebourg and many other sieges.

By comparison, Young Henry had nothing to show for himself. He had only the fact that he was the eldest son of his father. He did not reign in Anjou, Normandy, or England. His younger brother Geoffrey had Brittany to call his own, and John had Ireland.

Young Henry had no territories or armies. All he owned was his future title as head of the Plantagenet dynasty. Among the lords and barons of the empire, this title carried very little importance and won little respect.

In June 1183, Young Henry took a fateful decision. He wanted to shock his entire family, the nobles of the realm, the people, and the church. He wanted money for arms, men, and horses. He rode south to the sacred shrine of Rocamadour.

For centuries, pilgrims had walked and rode to Rocamadour. Hidden away in this place was the sword of Roland. This legendary crusader had fought the Muslims in Spain. While returning to France, he was ambushed and killed by Basques in the Pyrenees Mountains.

Over the years, pilgrims had come to pay their respects at the shrine. They left money and jewelry at the shrine as a tribute to Roland's great courage.

Henry had other ideas. He demanded a payment from the keepers of the shrine. After collecting the money, he rode back to the north. On the way, a fever overcame him. He suffered from dysentery. The local people believed he was suffering the vengeance of God for looting Rocamadour.

In the village of Martel, he stopped to take shelter at a peasant's house. Realizing that he might not survive, Henry asked for men of the church to come to Martel and hear his confession. Soon a bishop and an abbot arrived at his bedside.

Henry sent a message to his father, asking the king to ride south so they could work out a truce. The king refused, fearing that his son was laying a trap. As a token of his forgiveness, however, he sent back the messengers with a ring from his own finger.

Young Henry felt death coming. Sadness and regret came over him for his rebellion against his father. He fell to the floor before a priest who had come to hear his last confession. Henry laid his head on the bare floor. The priest counseled him to prepare him for a final judgment by God.

THE PLANTAGENET NAME

The father of Henry II, Geoffrey of Anjou, had a curious habit. He often wore a sprig of the broom plant in his hat. He loved the appearance of the plant so much that he adopted it as his emblem. The name of the plant, *planta genesta*, led to Geoffrey's second given name, *Plantagenet*.

Historians have named Geoffrey's family and dynasty Plantagenet. But in fact, the family never used the name themselves until the fifteenth century. They had no surnames, only nicknames and titles, as was customary for the nobles of the Middle Ages. Henry II was known as Henry FitzEmpress. Richard's brother was John Lackland—as he had no hereditary lands to call his own. The second son of Henry II knew himself only as Richard, count of Poitou.

In the fourteenth century, a French writer composed *Kynge Rycharde Cuer de Lyon*. This romance, a long poem of legendary deeds, told the legend of how Richard had once killed a lion by tearing out its heart. This poem gave rise to Richard's nickname of *coeur de lion*–the Lion Heart.

The priest demanded that Henry take his father's ring from his finger. By this action, he would approach the gates of heaven with no worldly treasure. He would prove to God that he had left behind his ambition for gold and riches. Henry agreed—but try as he might, he could not get the ring from his finger. He saw this as a symbol of his father's forgiveness.

Soon afterward, Henry the Younger died at the age of twenty-eight. His dying wish was to be buried in the town of Rouen, in Normandy. A procession brought his body to Grandmont, a monastery that Henry had recently looted. There his funeral took place. When the procession reached Le Mans, the bishop of that town stopped it. He asked that Henry's body be laid to rest in his town.

In the meantime, messengers brought the news to King Henry and to Richard. Richard was now the eldest living son of King Henry and the heir to the Angevin empire. For King Henry, this was a very serious setback. He was anxious that no member of his family grow too powerful. He knew that Richard, with his money and his men at arms, could easily seize the Angevin domain on the continent, from Aquitaine to Normandy. He could also, if he wished, defeat his brothers, Geoffrey and John, and usurp his father's title and throne.

The Plantagenet dynasty prepared again for violent conflict.

Heir to the Angevin Throne

THE DEATH OF HENRY THE YOUNGER IN 1183 left Richard as the eldest living son and heir of Henry II. The king had not expected this. He knew Richard was the strongest of his sons. But he wanted a balance of power in the family.

The death of Young Henry upset this balance. For this reason, Henry now schemed to restore his own authority. He wanted to be the unquestioned head of the family. He also wanted to block Richard's ambitions.

The three sons of Henry rode to Angers to meet with the king. Henry demanded that Richard, Geoffrey, and John make peace among themselves. He asked Richard to surrender control of Poitou and Aquitaine to John. He explained that John would do Richard homage for these rich lands. In addition, Henry would name Richard as the next king of England.

In trade for the southern domains, Henry offered Richard new titles. Richard would become the count of

Anjou and the duke of Normandy. These were Henry's homelands, however. Until his death, he would remain in control of them. Like the younger Henry, Richard would have to rule Normandy and Anjou as Henry's vassal.

Richard did not want trouble with his father. He did not give an answer. He rode away from Angers, to the south. A company of loyal knights and ministers rode with him.

Richard knew that he owed his father the respect of a son. But he did not want to become a vassal for the lands he held. He had no interest in Anjou or Normandy. He had no interest in England and no desire to rule it. His home was in the duchy of Aquitaine.

When Richard arrived in Poitiers, he sent a message back to Henry. He would not give up an inch of his land. He would stay in Aquitaine, as lord and master. He would pay homage to nobody. Richard prepared his knights and fortified his castles. He knew that another war with his brothers was coming.

While still a prisoner in England's Windsor Castle, Eleanor, Richard's mother, heard the news of the council in Angers. Henry's plans to give Aquitaine to John surprised and angered her. She did not want Richard, her favorite son, to lose his southern domains. She also believed that the king of France was plotting to seize Aquitaine from the Plantagenets. She believed Richard was much more capable than John of resisting this threat.

A Suspicious Prince

Alais, the sister of King Philip, was still living in England under King Henry's watchful eye. Henry had not forgotten

THE DARK LEGEND OF
THE PLANTAGENETS

There were many legends and stories about the Plantagenet family. The people of the Angevin lands knew these stories well. They had some suspicions and fears about the family that ruled over them.

One of Richard's ancestors was Count Fulk, the count of Anjou and a king of Jerusalem. He married a strange bride who had some odd habits. For some reason, she felt great fear whenever in a Christian church. During the mass, when the priest held up consecrated bread, she always fled in terror.

One day, the count ordered four of his knights to stand on her cloak, to prevent her from leaving. When the consecrated bread appeared, she screamed in terror, ripped her cloak from her body, and crashed through a window to escape.

Many people said this woman was in fact Melusine, the daughter of the devil. It was from her, according to this legend, that Richard and Henry and the other Plantagenets got their bad tempers.

his old promise to have Alais and Richard married. But he had no intention whatsoever of keeping this promise.

If Alais married Richard, then Richard would become the brother-in-law of King Philip. The two men would become allies through the marriage. At any time, Richard could ask for the help of the French king and army. He would be even more of a threat to Henry's authority.

Richard saw things differently. After the council at Angers, he felt even more suspicious of his father. Richard could see that Henry was trying to cut him down to size. The old king had done the same thing to Young Henry. His father's actions had turned Young Henry into a troublesome and violent rebel. The rebellion had ended with Young Henry's death.

Richard believed an alliance with France might help him keep control of Aquitaine. The best way would be to consent to the marriage with Alais, after all.

Henry got wind of Richard's plan. He agreed to meet King Philip and try to reach a truce with him. In December 1183, Henry and Philip met at Gisors. Under the branches of an ancient elm tree, the two kings argued over their rights and territory.

Henry finally made a bold offer. He would have John, not Richard, marry Alais. He also offered to pay Philip homage for all the Angevin lands on the continent. He would become the vassal of Philip in Normandy, Anjou, and Aquitaine.

The agreement shocked everyone—especially Richard. His worst suspicions were coming true. His father wanted John to inherit the Angevin crown. By paying homage to Philip, Henry was doing something even worse. He was taking land out of his sons' control, and claiming it as his own. If he succeeded, Richard would lose his authority in Aquitaine.

GEOFFREY IN PARIS

In the meantime, the ambitious Geoffrey had moved to Paris, the capital of France. Geoffrey had made an alliance with King Philip of France. Both men wanted to help each other. Philip wanted to extend the borders of his kingdom to the west. Geoffrey wanted control of the county of Anjou, which bordered his domain of Brittany.

Philip offered the help of the French army to conquer this territory. Eventually, Philip hoped, France could take control of Anjou by marriage or by war. This would split the Angevin empire in two. It would pave the way for French mastery of lands that now belonged to the Plantagenet dynasty.

Geoffrey set out from Paris in the fall of 1184. He joined his brother John and led an army of mercenaries into Poitou. The brothers attacked Richard's lands and castles. Richard counterattacked, leading his men into Brittany, Geoffrey's territory. Again, peasants and townspeople suffered while the members of the Plantagenet family settled their differences with war and looting.

King Henry, angered by this new outbreak, summoned his three sons to England. In late November, Geoffrey, John, and Richard arrived at Westminster, a royal palace near London. Henry also had Eleanor brought to Westminster.

Henry wanted Eleanor to give her blessing to his plan to have Richard give up Aquitaine to John. He knew his sons respected their mother. They might defy him, but they would listen to her—and perhaps take her advice.

At a formal ceremony, the three surviving Plantagenet sons bowed in homage to their father. They gave each other the traditional "kiss of peace." The family dined together at a magnificent banquet. Musicians and jesters provided entertainment. Parents and brothers talked and joked. All of their differences seemed to be settled.

But when Henry announced his plans to Eleanor, she angrily refused to consent. She wanted Richard to remain master of Poitou and Aquitaine. He was her favorite son, the only one she really trusted. Henry's plan had backfired.

Henry did not give up his efforts to tame his powerful son. In the spring of 1185, he summoned Eleanor to Normandy. He had already allowed his queen some freedom from her captivity. She could travel in England and on the Continent. But he kept his eyes on her, through spies loyal to him. He knew Eleanor opposed his plans for Richard and could not be trusted.

He then sent a demand to Richard. He wanted Richard to surrender Poitou to his mother. It was she who had been master of this territory, well before Richard was born. Now that she was a free woman, he should now return it to her.

Richard agreed. He would not oppose his own mother for control of her land. He surrendered Poitou as well as Aquitaine. He rode north to his father's court in Rouen, the capital of Normandy. He stayed at Henry's palace, paying his father due respect. He patiently waited for the right moment to take his vengeance.

BROKEN PROMISES

In the meantime, Geoffrey was living in a fine palace in Paris. He held court and plotted with King Philip against his own father. Philip continued sending messages to Henry about Alais. For the honor of his dynasty, Philip wanted the marriage of Richard and Alais to take place.

In March 1186, Philip met with Henry and offered a new agreement: Alais would marry Richard immediately. As her dowry, the king of France would offer Richard the Vexin. This was an important borderland between Normandy and France.

Henry agreed to the treaty. He accepted the offer of the Vexin. But he continued to put off the marriage of Richard and Alais. In fact he had no intention of seeing his eldest son married to the sister of the king of France.

To keep Richard occupied, Henry ordered his son to ride south, to fight the hostile count of Toulouse. This count had always been a thorn in the side of the Plantagenets. He raided frontier territories and defied the Plantagenets as much as possible. Richard, eager for war and feeling himself under Henry's watchful eye, obeyed his father. He invaded the troublesome count's lands, which lay east of Aquitaine. He soon defeated the count's forces and brought him to heel.

RICHARD AND PHILIP

In the summer of 1186, Geoffrey was still living in Paris. He joined the French king for feasts and ceremonies.

He allied his own forces to those of France. He waited for an opportunity to seize land and titles from his brothers.

But on August 19, all Geoffrey's plans and dreams came to an end. While riding in a tournament, he suffered a fall from his horse. The horse trampled him, and Geoffrey soon died from his injuries. The French king, in a show of respect, had Geoffrey buried in the cathedral of Notre Dame.

The death of Geoffrey struck a blow to the king of France. Still angered by Henry's refusal to allow the marriage of Richard and Alais, he demanded that Henry return the Vexin to French control. Philip also welcomed Richard to his court in Paris.

Philip and Richard became the best of friends in Paris. They rode together, dined together, and spent hours in conversation and plotting. They had many mutual interests—as well as a mutual enemy: King Henry II.

Philip let Richard in on an important secret. Henry wanted John, not Richard, to marry Alais. He planned to have John allied to France, and to inherit the Angevin domains. He planned to have John become the new duke of Aquitaine.

Richard knew or suspected much of this information already. But all of his anger and frustration now reached a boiling point. He swore to ally his forces with Philip's and fight his own father.

DEFEAT IN THE HOLY LAND

In the late summer of 1187, terrible news reached Europe. The Christian crusaders had met the Muslim armies at the Horns of Hattin, near the Sea of Galilee. The Muslim commander was Saladin, a brilliant military leader. The Christian general was Guy of Lusignan, the king of Jerusalem. He was the brother of Geoffrey of Lusignan, one of Richard's vassals.

Saladin had vowed to recapture Jerusalem from the Christians. At Hattin, Saladin utterly destroyed the Christian army. He spared the lives of only a few Christians, including his prisoner Guy of Lusignan. In October 1187, the Muslims arrived at the walls of Jerusalem. They soon captured the city.

The Christians of Jerusalem fell into despair. Many shaved their heads as a sign of fear and sorrow. But Saladin spared their lives. He took thousands of them as prisoners and held them for ransom.

The archbishop of Tyre, Josias, set out for Europe. In October, he reached Italy. He told Pope Urban III of the capture of Jerusalem. When he heard the news, the elderly pope fell ill and soon died—as many said, of grief. The next pope, Gregory VIII, quickly proclaimed a new crusade. He also died, less than two months later.

Archbishop Josias continued his journey to France. Meanwhile, the church declared that it was now the duty of all Christian knights and rulers to lay down their arms. They must agree to a truce. They must take the fight to the

After Saladin (above) and his army captured Jerusalem, Richard I prepared to join the Crusade against the Muslim forces.

Muslims. They must gather their armies and sail away from Europe, and save the holy city.

Moved by the terrible news from the Holy Land, Philip and Henry decided to make peace. According to medieval custom, the rivals agreed to a Truce of God. They agreed to quit their fighting while a crusade was underway.

Richard also prepared to take the cross and leave on Crusade. He saw a bleak future for himself in Europe. His father, he knew, would never allow him to prosper as an Angevin ruler. Perhaps he could win a more important victory in the Holy Land.

In the cathedral of Tours, Richard vowed to undertake a crusade. If he was successful in this Crusade, he knew he would win honor and glory. He would also become the unquestioned master of the Angevin empire. No one would challenge his lawful right to inherit his father's titles and land.

His father had other ideas. He feared Richard's new friendship with Philip. He plotted with the count of Toulouse to attack Richard. He also encouraged the nobles of Aquitaine to rise in rebellion against Richard.

Richard collected a large army. He defeated the count's forces. He arrived at the gates of Toulouse itself and prepared to reduce the city to ruins. In the meantime, Philip attacked the Angevin lands and was in turn attacked by Henry II's army.

In early 1188, the kings of France and England again made a truce. They were met by Archbishop Josias of Tyre. The archbishop described how the Muslims were seizing the holy places and killing Christians. The archbishop preached the crusade to the two kings, demanding that they leave as soon as possible.

Philip and Henry again vowed to take the cross and leave on Crusade. Henry sailed back to England. He raised money to pay for the Crusade. The people of England reluctantly paid this "Saladin Tithe." It amounted to 10 percent of their income. The priests and bishops of the church collected the Saladin Tithe. Those who did not pay suffered excommunication by the church. Those who went on a Crusade were excused from paying.

The two kings' promise to keep the truce lasted until the spring. Philip attacked Henry's lands, and Henry sailed back across the English Channel to take his revenge. The kings agreed to meet once more in Gisors.

This time, Henry and Philip could not make peace. They argued and accused each other of treachery. They parted, vowing to make war until the other should surrender. Philip ordered the ancient elm tree of Gisors to be cut down. There would be no more peaceful councils between the two men.

THE DEFEAT OF HENRY II

Richard saw his opportunity in the war between England and France. He allied with King Philip. From Henry, he demanded his rightful inheritance: the Angevin crown. He demanded Anjou and other territories. He also announced that he would marry Alais.

Henry refused these demands. He vowed to stop the marriage. But he was approaching old age. He was fifty-five years old and growing weak. Many illnesses beset the king. The years of strife and fighting had taken their toll. He finally asked for a truce with Philip.

The truce lasted through the winter and spring. Then, in the summer of 1189, the French armies went on the rampage again. They invaded Henry's lands and destroyed several of his castles. Nobles who had been loyal to the

This tapestry shows King Henry II of England fleeing (right) Le Mans as King Philip II of France storms the city.

king deserted him. Henry was forced to run from one stronghold to another, to avoid capture by the French. Richard and Philip attacked Henry at his court in Le Mans, driving Henry out of the city.

At his heels was Richard, his son. At the head of a powerful army, Richard chased his father through the green hills of Normandy. Exhausted, Henry sued for peace, and surrendered the important city of Tours on the Loire River. In July, Henry took refuge in the castle of Chinon. He took to a sickbed and grew weak. Too tired and ill to fight, he agreed to surrender to Philip.

Henry met the French king on the road from Chinon. Philip demanded that Henry surrender all of his lands on the continent to Richard. He must surrender Alais and go on Crusade within the year.

Henry agreed to all of the terms. There was no fight left in the king. He was old and frail. He had finally met defeat at the hands of the king of France. Worse, his own sons had betrayed him.

As a token of his agreement, he offered the kiss of peace to Richard. Father and son awkwardly embraced. Henry may have lost to his son but he would never forgive him. As he pulled away, Henry whispered into Richard's ear, "God grant that I may not die until I have had a fitting revenge on you."[1]

Henry rode back in great pain and bitterness to the castle of Chinon. Only a few servants and knights stayed with him. The master of the greatest empire in Europe now had only a castle and a few loyal followers. Then a servant brought him terrible news. His youngest son John had helped Richard's rebellion. The son he believed most loyal to him had proved to be a traitor. On July 6, 1189, Henry died in a lonely bedchamber.

When he heard the news of his father's death, Richard rode to Chinon. He climbed the stone steps to his father's room and knelt to say a prayer at the foot of the bed. According to witnesses: ". . . blood began to flow from the nostrils of the dead King, and ceased not to flow so long as his son remained there, as if his spirit were angered at Richard's approach."[2]

EPITAPH FOR KING HENRY II

Richard brought the body of his father to the abbey of Fontrevault. The king was buried in the church choir, at the eastern end of the abbey. Artisans built a stone tomb and an effigy of the king. An epitaph honored and remembered the king:

> I am Henry the King. To me
> Divers realms were subject.
> I was duke and count of many provinces.
> Eight feet of ground is now enough for me,
> Whom many kingdoms failed to satisfy.
> Who reads these lines, let him reflect
> Upon the narrowness of death.
> And in my case behold
> The image of our mortal lot.
> This scanty tomb doth now suffice
> For whom the Earth was not enough.[3]

The war with Henry had left Richard with a sense of loss and regret. He brought his father's body to the abbey of Fontrevault. He said a prayer over the tomb. He was now the ruler of the Angevin realm and the king of England. But for the sake of his soul, and for the honor and glory of victory, his first desire was to go on Crusade.

THE KING OF ENGLAND

IN 1189, ON THE DEATH OF HENRY II, COUNT Richard of Poitou became the king of England. Richard inherited all of his father's possessions. He was now the ruler in England, Anjou, Normandy, and Aquitaine. He led the largest and wealthiest state in Europe.

Eleanor had been living in Winchester Castle. After hearing the news of Henry's death, she rode out from her castle. Richard had given her authority to act as his regent. Until his crowning ceremony, her word was law in England.

Eleanor met with the barons of the realm, to hear their assurances of loyalty to Richard. She also freed some of Henry's prisoners from their English jails. Many of them were peasants who had been jailed for poaching in the royal forests. She asked the English people to support Richard as the new king. She wrote a decree and had criers announce it throughout the realm: ". . . [E]very freeman in the whole realm must swear that he would bear fealty to the Lord Richard, lord of England, in life and limb and earthly honour as his liege lord, against all men and women, living or dead, and that they would be answerable to him and help him to keep his peace and justice in all things."[1]

RICHARD ARRIVES IN ENGLAND

Soon afterward, Richard sailed across the English Channel. He arrived at Portsmouth on August 12, 1189. He rode to the royal castle at Winchester to greet his mother. He then went to the underground treasure vaults of his father.

Richard had important plans, and he needed money. The first vault he opened was a disappointment, holding only one hundred thousand silver marks.[2] Believing the vaults had been robbed, he angrily summoned Ranulf de Glanville to his presence.

Under harsh questioning, Ranaulf revealed that Henry had been keeping a secret vault. Richard demanded the keys. Ranaulf quickly handed them over.

Richard discovered nearly a million marks of silver as well as gold and precious stones in the secret vault. Henry had been carefully guarding this treasure. Only a few people knew that it even existed.

Now that his father was dead, Richard claimed this horde of money, gold, and gems for himself. He had other ways of raising money. His new chancellor, William Longchamp, set to work raising taxes. Longchamp himself had to pay three thousand pounds for his office.[3] Richard and Longchamp sold offices, titles, land, and royal castles.

The new king declared, "I would sell London itself if I could find a buyer."[4]

He believed this hoard would allow him to realize his greatest ambition. He could pay and equip a powerful army. The army would help him succeed in a crusade to the Holy Land. His success, he was certain, would bring him glory in the eyes of Christians everywhere, for all time.

LEAVING ON A CRUSADE

Richard would not stay long in England. He had little interest in ruling this country. He would be a crusader. The treasure of his father, King Henry II, would allow him to raise an army, collect a fleet of ships, and sail to the Holy Land. There he would defeat the Muslims and capture the holy city of Jerusalem. The city would return to the Christians—thanks to him. His victory against the infidels would bring him honor and glory all over the world.

Richard knew he would be away from England for a long time, and that he had to safeguard his kingdom. He wanted to be sure that his power as king would be safe from scheming ministers and relatives. The most dangerous, he knew, was his half brother, Geoffrey.

Richard took steps against Geoffrey, who was the illegitimate son of Henry II and a prostitute. He removed Geoffrey from his post as chancellor of England. Richard named Geoffrey to a lesser post, as the new archbishop of York. As a condition, however, Geoffrey had to stay out of England for three years.

For his brother John, Richard simply offered a huge bribe. He gave him the lordship of eight castles and the authority over six earldoms in England. But John would also have to stay on the continent for a period of three years.

John had grown up with no inheritance and no land of his own. Richard knew him to be ambitious, a brother who would do anything for power and wealth. He believed that his gift to John would settle matters between them. But Richard did not realize how ambitious his brother really was.

Before he left on Crusade, Richard wanted to settle his marriage. He had lost interest in Alais, the princess of France. Instead, he agreed to marry Berengaria of Navarre. Berengaria was the sister of Sancho the Strong, prince of Navarre, and the daughter of Sancho the Wise, the king of Navarre. This small kingdom in northern Spain bordered Richard's lands in Aquitaine.

Richard had first seen Berengaria during a tournament in Pampeluna, the capital of Navarre. She was a quiet and shy young woman, with dark hair and eyes. Richard's mother Eleanor had proposed the marriage to her son, and Richard now accepted the idea.

The marriage would be useful to Richard. A marriage to Berengaria would ally his realm with Navarre. If the count of Toulouse or any other lord gave trouble in Aquitaine, Sancho the Wise would help. Richard wanted to protect Aquitaine. For him, the duchy was the most vital possession in the Angevin realm.

THE UNLUCKY DAY

The coronation of Richard as king of England took place on September 3, 1189. Thousands of onlookers attended the solemn ceremony at Westminster Abbey. Four men held a silk canopy over Richard's head as he entered the abbey church and walked toward the altar.

Bishops, archbishops, princes, and nobles walked in front and behind. Holding aloft silken cushions, the men carried symbols of the crown: a royal cap, golden spurs, ceremonial scepters and swords, and a golden crown.

At the altar, Richard took an oath to protect the church and to uphold justice and the traditions of his kingdom. Archbishop Baldwin of Canterbury anointed Richard with holy oil. Richard then stepped forward and dressed in the king's robes. To the cheers of the crowd, he took his place on the throne of England.

Coronation day was an occasion for feasting at court and celebration in the streets of London. The people closed their shops and left work. The crowning of a new king was a rare event, a highlight in the life of every English citizen.

For some, a coronation could also be violent and dangerous. During the ceremonies, a group of Jewish merchants appeared at the doors of Westminster Abbey. The Jews had not been allowed to attend the ceremony. Richard was a crusader, as well as a king, and non-Christians were not welcome. Nevertheless, these Jews had come to offer gifts and pay their respects.

THE DISMAL DAY

Richard didn't care much for old superstitions. He selected September 3 as the date of his coronation. Known as Egyptian Day, this particular date had a bad reputation. In ancient astrology, two days of every month were considered to be unlucky. In the Norman French spoken by Richard they were *dis mal* (evil days), the root of the modern English word *dismal*.

A group of Richard's courtiers took hold of the Jews and threw them into the street. A clerk, Roger of Hoveden, witnessed this event. He wrote about it in his chronicle, *The Annals*:

> While the king was seated at table, the chief men of the Jews came to offer presents to him, but as they had been forbidden the day before to come to the king's court on the day of the coronation, the common people, with scornful eye and insatiable heart, rushed upon the Jews and stripped them, and then scourging them, cast them forth out of the king's hall. A mob then surrounded and attacked the visitors. The riots spread throughout England in the next few days. Christians killed hundreds of Jews and looted their property.[5]

In the city of York, the Jews boarded themselves up in their homes and fought off their attackers. When they could no longer stop the assault, the men killed their wives and children and cut their own throats.[6]

On his coronation day, Richard I received the crown of England.

SETTING OUT ON CRUSADE

Richard did not spend much time in England. For him, the kingdom was unimportant. He did not speak English, the language of the common people, and he did not care for the cold, rainy weather. His ambitions also ranged much farther than France and the Angevin lands. He did not concern himself with the many squabbles of Europe.

Instead, Richard wanted to keep the promise made to his father on Henry's deathbed. He would leave on a Crusade. He would assemble an army and a grand fleet of ships. He would recapture the holy city of Jerusalem from the Muslim infidels.

Richard believed victory in Palestine would earn him eternal glory and honor. Troubadours would sing his praises. The church would bless him and his heirs. The church and the people would forget his sins, especially his disloyalty to his father.

Richard would not fight alone. King Philip of France had also promised to go on Crusade. The emperor of Germany, Frederick Barbarossa, would join the battle with a large army of infantry and cavalry. Barbarossa was already marching this army through eastern Europe. He would soon reach Palestine.

Richard sent Archbishop Baldwin ahead, to the city of Acre in Palestine. With a small company of knights and soldiers, Baldwin was to assist in the siege of Acre. The Muslims had captured this fortress, on the coast of the Mediterranean Sea, after the Battle of Hattin. Baldwin would prepare the Christian camp at Acre for Richard's arrival.

Richard appointed trusted men to run the kingdom and the Angevin domains. In the spring of 1190, he left England. He sent a huge fleet of ships south to the Mediterranean Sea. He had carefully planned their voyage. They would sail to the ports of southern France. In the meantime, he would march across France with his army.

He had agreed to meet King Philip at the town of Vezelay, the site of a wealthy abbey. The two kings would continue to the seacoast and then board their armies on ships. They would regroup on the island of Sicily and sail for the Holy Land as soon as possible. They wanted to reach Palestine before winter. Sailing on the Mediterranean in winter was very dangerous.

Richard reached the port of Marseille in southern France on July 31, 1190. He discovered that the fleet of ships from England had not yet arrived. The sailors and crusaders had been attacking Jews and Muslims in Lisbon. The king of Portugal had imprisoned several hundred crusaders. Richard would have to wait for his ships.

RENDEZVOUS IN SICILY

Archbishop Baldwin reached Palestine shortly after Richard arrived in Marseille. Baldwin found the Christians camped in sight of the walls of Acre. They were not attacking the city. Instead, they were squabbling among themselves over rights and privileges, just as they did in Europe.

Baldwin felt confident that Richard would settle these quarrels. He also believed Richard to be the best military leader of all the Christian rulers. He impatiently waited for the king's arrival.

In the meantime, Eleanor had left with a large court for Navarre. She wanted to formally request the hand of Berengaria as Richard's wife. For Sancho the Wise, the king of Navarre, Richard's proposal offered an ideal match. His dynasty would be allied with one of the most powerful monarchs in Europe. He readily agreed to the marriage.

With Berengaria in her company, Eleanor then set off for Marseilles. When they reached the port, they found that Richard had already left. Too impatient to wait for his ships, he had decided to journey overland. He marched down the Italian peninsula, to the island of Sicily. Eleanor and Berengaria followed the king.

In the meantime, Richard's ships finally caught up with him. As Richard marched to Sicily, the ships sailed just offshore to accompany the king. Whenever possible, Richard kept on dry land. Sea travel always made him very sick.

In his royal squadron, Richard made the short voyage across the Strait of Messina on September 22. One eyewitness described the scene:

> The populace rushed out eagerly to behold him, crowding along the shore. And lo, on the horizon

they saw a fleet of innumerable galleys, filling the Straits, and then, still far off, they could hear the shrill sound of trumpets. As the galleys came nearer they could see that they were painted in different colours and hung with shields glittering in the sun. . . . Then, with trumpet peals ringing in their ears, the onlookers beheld what they had been waiting for: the King of England, magnificently dressed and standing on a raised platform, so that he could see and be seen.[7]

On Sicily, Richard found his restless troops already engaged in combat. Many of the Sicilians were Greeks, nicknamed griffons. They belonged to the eastern Christian church, which did not support the Crusades. The Greeks were fighting with the French crusaders under Philip's control. There were frequent clashes in the streets, robberies, and murder.

Philip and Richard also had the matter of Richard's marriage contract to settle. Philip still expected Richard to marry his sister, Alais. Richard wanted Philip to release him from this obligation. But the two kings could not come to an agreement.

Their quarrel was a bad sign for the Crusade they were about to lead together. In the end, Philip refused to let Richard out of the agreement. He left Messina furious with his fellow crusader.

BATTLES ON SICILY

When Richard arrived in Sicily, the island was under the rule of King Tancred. He was a short, violent, and greedy man. He had seized power after the recent death of King William, the husband of Richard's favorite sister, Joanna.

Richard was supposed to be crusading against the Muslims in the Holy Land. But he stopped his voyage to settle affairs with Tancred. Richard believed that William had intended to offer the crusaders valuable gifts: ships, food, weapons, silken tents, and a treasure in golden plate and cups. He also believed that William had settled a gift of land on Joanna by his will. He was angry with Tancred for preventing her from taking possession of it.

At the same time, the English soldiers were causing trouble in Messina. The Greeks looked on the Englishmen as foreigners and invaders. In the town markets, the merchants refused to sell the English any food or wares. The Sicilians assaulted English soldiers. Outside the walls, several deadly battles broke out.

Richard angrily confronted Tancred. He collected his men and attacked La Bagnara, a fortress on the seacoast near Messina. After seizing the fortress, he brought Joanna there for safekeeping. He then attacked and captured a monastery, allowing his soldiers to use it as a barracks.

When the attacks on the English continued, Richard vowed vengeance. He collected a small army of his best men and rampaged through Messina, killing hundreds of townspeople. In the meantime, the French army of Philip did nothing to stop the fighting or interfere. They did nothing as the English soldiers looted shops and burned houses.

Richard raised his banner over the city walls, signifying that he was now the master of it. Unable to combat the

Like Richard, Tancred was also a crusader.

powerful crusading army, Tancred fled to the mainland of Italy and asked for a truce.

Richard agreed to stop the fighting. He demanded that Tancred hand over the land and valuables promised to the Angevins. Tancred agreed to pay forty thousand ounces of gold. Half the gold belonged to Joanna. Richard could use the other half on his crusade.

The two men then signed a truce. They promised to keep the peace between Greeks and Englishmen. Richard restored some of the property looted by his men. He also promised to defend Tancred should Sicily ever be invaded. The two men sealed their agreement with a marriage promise. A daughter of Tancred was to marry Arthur of Brittany, Richard's nephew.

The agreement brought peace to Sicily. But it was now too late in the year to sail for the Holy Land. The armies of Richard and Philip spent a long and restless winter in Sicily. The soldiers grew bored, while the two kings wrangled over Richard's promise to marry Alais.

In March 1191, Richard and Philip agreed to settle the matter. Philip let Richard out of his obligation to marry Alais. Philip settled the territory of the Vexin and its stronghold of Gisors on Richard during his lifetime. If he died without an heir, the territory would again become French property.

In the meantime, Eleanor and Berengaria were approaching Sicily. When Philip heard the news, he prepared to leave the island immediately. He felt humiliated by Richard's refusal to marry his sister. He could not stand the thought of sharing a table or a city with the woman who had taken his sister's place. On the day before the two women arrived at Messina, Philip ordered his men aboard their ships. He sailed away from Sicily to the east.

ARRIVAL IN CYPRUS

As soon as Eleanor and Berengaria arrived, Richard felt impatient to leave. He ordered his own crusader fleet, two hundred ships strong, to set sail in April 1191.[8] Richard commanded the fleet from his flagship. He sailed to the Greek islands of Crete and Rhodes, off the coast of Turkey. Then he set out for Cyprus.

On the way, a heavy storm broke up the fleet. Several ships, including the ship carrying Berengaria and Richard's sister Joanna, sailed off course. This group reached Cyprus ahead of the main fleet.

Greeks had been settling in Cyprus for more than two thousand years. Since the fall of the western Roman Empire, the island had belonged to the Byzantine Empire. But in 1185, the Byzantine prince Isaac Comnenus had seized the island for himself. Comnenus defied the Byzantine emperor and made the island his private domain. He ruled the people of Cyprus with great cruelty.[9]

Comnenus feared the crusader army approaching his island. He knew this force was much larger than the army he commanded. He was determined to keep the crusaders away from Cyprus.

The small fleet carrying Berengaria and Joanna arrived at the port of Amathus, on the southern coast of Cyprus. Comnenus sent his armies to meet them. He raised defenses against the fleet. He ordered his men to capture any of Richard's men caught on land and throw them into prison. He did not even allow the crusaders to search his island for fresh water.

Then Comnenus sent gifts out to the ship carrying Berengaria and Joanna. He invited the two women ashore as his guests. His invitation was not done out of kindness. Comnenus wanted to make Richard's sister and fiancée his hostages.

Suspicious, Joanna and Berengaria turned down the invitation. Soon afterward, Richard arrived with the main crusader fleet. When he learned what Comnenus had been up to, Richard grew angry. He ordered his ships to drop their anchors. He sent his men ashore immediately. Without waiting for his horses, he attacked Amathus. The town soon fell to Richard's crossbowmen and his knights, who were fighting on foot.

THE NEW QUEEN OF ENGLAND

Richard then attended to some important business. On May 12, he married Berengaria in the Chapel of Saint George in Amathus. That same day, a bishop crowned Berengaria as the new queen of England. A feast to celebrate the wedding and the coronation lasted three full days.

After the celebrations, Richard formed up his army and marched it north. In a few days, he reached the walls of Nicosia, the capital city. The people of Cyprus, unhappy

In the midst of a military campaign on Cyprus, Richard married Berengaria.

under the rule of the cruel Comnenus, helped the crusader army.

Richard and a band of mounted knights entered the city. They forced Comnenus to flee into his stronghold within the walls of Nicosia. Comnenus did not even attempt to fight. He asked for a truce and a parley (meeting). At the parley, the tyrant of Cyprus agreed to do homage to Richard as his vassal.

Comnenus had no intention of serving Richard faithfully, according to feudal custom. Immediately after the ceremony of homage, he selected the fastest horse in his stable and rode away from Nicosia. Comnenus then sent messengers to Saladin, the head of the Muslim army that had conquered Jerusalem. The tyrant of Cyprus offered to ally himself with Saladin and fight the crusaders.

For several weeks, Comnenus harried the crusader army. His men set ambushes and skirmished with Richard's troops in the mountains of northern Cyprus. Outnumbered, Comnenus knew he had no hope of defeating Richard in battle. If Richard arrived with a large number of troops, the Cypriots ran from the field.

Richard organized his men for an all-out attack.

Comnenus then retreated to the castle of Kantara, in the rugged Troodos Mountains of northern Cyprus. Before he could lead his men into battle, however, Richard fell ill.

He sent his vassal Guy of Lusignan into northern Cyprus to confront Isaac Comnenus. Lusignan was to defeat the Greeks and take Comnenus prisoner. If necessary, he was to kill the king of Cyprus.

In the meantime, Richard ordered all the men of Nicosia to shave off their beards. He disliked the Greek habit of growing beards. By this new law, he intended to humiliate his Greek subjects and make western Europeans out of them.

THE CONQUEST OF CYPRUS

On Richard's instructions, Guy of Lusignan marched an army of knights and infantry into northern Cyprus. His men attacked the castles of Isaac Comnenus.

Comnenus took his army to Nicosia, in the center of the island. He sent his wife and daughter to Kyrenia. This stronghold lay on a steep hill in the Troodos Mountains.

Comnenus then led his small army north to meet Richard. The two armies clashed at Tremithus. Richard had a powerful army of well-armed crusaders. He was ready for a long campaign in Palestine. Comnenus had only a few thousand soldiers on foot and horseback.

The battle was over quickly. Comnenus fled the battle-field with his men. He rode north to Kantara, intending to wait out the crusader army.

THE DEATH OF A CRUSADER

Frederick Barbarossa was the ruler of the Holy Roman Empire. He was dedicated to the cause of the Crusades. In 1189, he set out from Germany with a huge army.

The troops marched through eastern Europe and reached the Byzantine Empire. They crossed the Bosporus strait and arrived in Asia Minor. With Richard I of England and King Philip of France joining the Third Crusade, the Christian world was ready to reconquer the Holy Land.

But Barbarossa would never reach Palestine. While crossing the Saleph River, he fell from his horse. The shock of the water may have caused a heart attack. The heavy armor he was wearing dragged him down, underneath the surface. He drowned in water only a few feet deep.

The news of Frederick Barbarossa's death soon reached the Holy Land. The Muslims and their leader, Saladin, were overjoyed at the news. The Christians grew fearful and anxious. One of their most important leaders had accidentally drowned—a bad omen for the Crusade. Their best hope now lay in the skill and energy of Richard I of England.

Guy of Lusignan then captured Kyrenia. He took Comnenus' daughter as a hostage. The news that his daughter was now a captive frightened Isaac Comnenus.

The tyrant of Cyprus came to Richard on bended knee. He surrendered his island and begged for pardon. Richard could appoint any ruler he chose. Comnenus only asked one favor: not to be put in chains of iron.

Richard agreed, and put Comnenus in chains of silver. Richard then made Cyprus his own. He knew the island would be an important possession for the crusaders. It lay just off the coast of Palestine and was easy to defend. The new ruler of Cyprus raided the treasury of the island and used the money to pay his men and buy them horses and weapons.

Richard had good reasons for the capture of Cyprus. In the future, the income from the island would help pay for his battles in the Holy Land. He could use it as a base for his fleets and armies. If they needed to, the Christians could retreat to Cyprus for safety.

Richard wasted no time after his victory in Cyprus. He assembled his fleet again. His knights, archers, and foot soldiers brought their stores and weapons aboard the ships. The fleet set sail for the Holy Land.

IN THE HOLY LAND

ON JUNE 7, 1191, AFTER THE SHORT VOYAGE FROM the island of Cyprus, Richard's fleet arrived off the coast of Palestine. It had been more than a year since Richard I had left England. The crusading king was ready and very eager for battle.

He was facing a worthy opponent. Salah al-Din, also known as Saladin today, was a leader of a Kurdish clan, the Ayyub. He seized control of Egypt in 1169. Five years later, he marched into Syria and captured Damascus. As the vizier, or ruler, of Egypt and Syria, he also led the strongest Muslim armies of Palestine.

Many Muslim nobles opposed Saladin's rule. They saw him as a usurper—someone who had stolen his power and titles. But Saladin was a skilled politician as well as a military leader. He answered by forming an army to fight the Christians. He declared war on the "Franks" (the name Muslims gave to the men from Europe).

In 1187, Saladin had crushed the Christian armies at the Battle of Hattin. Later that year, he captured Jerusalem. The Franks were driven out of Palestine, except for a few cities on the Mediterranean coast.

THE LIONHEART ARRIVES

Richard's first meeting with the enemy occurred even before he touched dry land. His fleet intercepted a Muslim supply ship. Richard ordered an immediate attack. The battle lasted several hours. In the end, the Muslim ship sank into the sea. There were very few survivors.

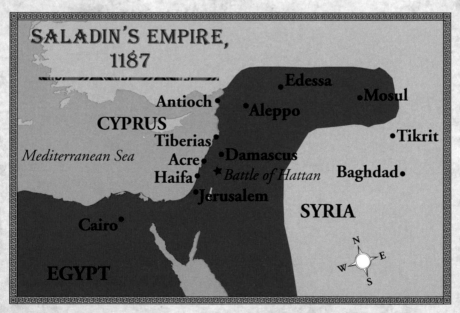

The land around Jerusalem was considered the Holy Land to Christians, Muslims, and Jews, many of whom were willing to fight for possession of it.

On the following day, Richard joined the European armies camped around the city of Acre. As he came ashore, the Christians greeted him with cheers.

The Christians were laying siege to the city, waiting for the Muslims to surrender and open the gates. But the walls of Acre were high and strong. Several thousand foot soldiers and archers defended the city. The siege had lasted nearly two years before the English king arrived.

The crusader army was divided, fighting under several leaders. Philip of France, Leopold of Austria, the duke of Burgundy, and Conrad of Montferrat all commanded their own men. Each of these leaders looked after their own interests. They were unable to cooperate with one another. Acre as well as Jerusalem remained in Muslim hands.

Conrad and Richard's vassal, Guy of Lusignan, were both contending for the title of king of Jerusalem. Even though Jerusalem was now under Saladin's control, Conrad and Guy hoped to some day liberate the city. Each thought he had the right to rule all of the Christians living in the Holy Land.

Conrad had married Isabella, the daughter of the last king of Jerusalem. Guy had married Sibylla, the king's elder daughter. When the old king had died, Guy claimed the crown and ruled for Sibylla. But after Sibylla's death, Conrad claimed the throne as his by right of marriage to the only surviving daughter.

Richard supported Guy's claim to the title. Guy was his vassal and the man he was sworn to support. But Conrad was a far better military leader. He had more supporters among the common soldiers as well as the nobles and princes. King Philip of France also supported Conrad's claim.

The rivalry between Guy de Lusignan and Conrad of Montferrat weakened the Christian army. The Europeans could not unite their forces to conquer Acre. Nor could they march on Jerusalem. They needed, above all, a good military commander. When Richard arrived, they took heart. All recognized Richard as the most able general among them.

BEFORE THE WALLS OF ACRE

Richard found Acre's surroundings a wasteland. The land was barren, strewn with litter, broken weapons, and charred trees. The bodies of horses and pack mules, dead of hunger or thirst, rotted in the hot sun. The Christian armies had destroyed orchards, burned fields, and seized livestock. Farmers had abandoned their estates and fled to the safety of the city.

Food and water were scarce. Diseases spread throughout the camps. Many of the soldiers, as well as thousands of people within Acre, had died during the siege. The Christians often fought among themselves over food, supplies, territory, and their feudal rights.

In the meantime, Saladin had set up a camp in the hills near the city. The Muslim general did not want to surrender the stronghold of Acre. Saladin's army harassed the Christians with night raids and ambushes.

Nevertheless, the arrival of Richard struck fear in the Muslim camp. His reputation as a brave and skilled warrior was already known to Saladin. One of Saladin's emirs (nobles) had the following warning for the Muslim leader: "Never have we seen his like; or met with his peer. He is ever foremost of the enemy at each onset; he is first as befits the pick and flower of knighthood. It is he who maims our folk. No one can resist him or rescue a captive from his hands."[1]

NEW HOPE FOR THE CHRISTIAN CAMP

Richard had sent Archbishop Baldwin of Canterbury ahead from Sicily to prepare the camp. But on landing at Acre, Richard discovered that Baldwin had taken sick and died. Hubert Walter had then taken the English force under his command. This capable and energetic man had imposed some order and discipline on the Englishmen.

Richard was pleased at Walter's achievement. He had much less respect for King Philip and the other commanders at the siege. Philip's actions in Sicily, and the way he had fled the island at the approach of Eleanor and Berengaria, made Richard feel contempt for the French king's leadership. In turn, Richard's own ability and charisma made the other European princes intensely jealous.

Richard gave the entire Christian camp new hope and confidence. He had brought thousands of men as reinforcements, as well as weapons, siege equipment, horses, and treasure. The men knew his reputation as a commander and his success at the siege of Taillebourg and other strongholds.

It was obvious that Richard had more energy and more skill in warfare than the other commanders. Richard also was offering higher pay to soldiers who would fight under his command. Many knights and foot soldiers were accepting his offer. The ranks of the English army grew. The French king and the other commanders lost men.

The Muslim camp heard the news of Richard's arrival with fear. They knew the fierce reputation of this king. They knew the Christian soldiers would fight well under his leadership. With the arrival of Richard and his powerful army, the siege of Acre had taken a turn for the worse for the Muslims.

AN OFFER OF SNOW

Shortly after his arrival, Richard came down with a serious illness. He grew exhausted, and his hair and fingernails fell out. A strange rash broke out on his skin, and he found that he could hardly stir from his bed.

But he knew that time was valuable. The siege could not wait for him to return to health. He ordered his men to carry him around the battlefield on a litter. From this mobile bed, Richard directed the fire of his archers. He coordinated the rain of arrows with blasts from his mangonels. These giant catapults hurled heavy stones at the walls of Acre.

Richard also ordered scaffolds built beside the city walls. These scaffolds rose higher than the battlements of Acre. They allowed the archers to direct their fire downward into the city.

The siege machines of the crusaders were designed to batter down even the strongest walls of cities.

Acre was larger and stronger than the fortress of Taillebourg. But Richard knew that sooner or later Acre would fall to the Christians. The sinking of the Muslim supply ship had dealt a heavy blow to the defenders of the city. The Christian army was surrounding Acre, preventing the Muslims from sending food and reinforcements into the city.

Richard sent messengers to Saladin, offering a truce. If the Muslims surrendered, their lives would be spared. Saladin refused, however, to agree to the truce. Nor would he meet with the English king. As long as the two sides were fighting a battle, Saladin saw no reason to talk to Richard.

During this time, Saladin expressed his hopes and dreams to a Muslim writer, Baha al-Din ibn Shaddad: "When by God's help not a Frank is left on this coast, I mean to divide my territories, and to charge [my successors] with my last commands; then, having taken leave of them, I will sail on this sea to its islands in pursuit of them, until there shall not remain on the face of this earth one unbeliever in God, or I will die in the attempt."[2]

But Saladin also had his own code of chivalry. He paid his respects to the English king as an equal. From the mountains where he camped, he sent down a gift of fruit and snow. It was a Muslim custom to mix the two ingredients to make a refreshing sweet, a kind of medieval ice cream. In return, Richard sent Saladin the gift of a slave. The siege of Acre continued, as the two leaders did their best to destroy each other.

CRACKS IN THE WALLS

The siege resumed with greater violence. Angered at the fact that many of his men had deserted to Richard's army, Philip planned a direct assault on Acre. He ordered his siege engines brought up to the walls. He sent his men to the walls with scaling ladders. He hoped to win the siege and greater honor for himself.

When Richard heard of the plan, he ordered his own men to remain in their tents. He believed that Philip would not succeed. The walls of Acre were still too strong. He did not want to lose any English soldiers in a hopeless assault.

As Richard had foreseen, Philip's attack was a total failure. The Muslims threw back his men from the walls with heavy losses. The Muslims then burst out from the gates of the city. They fought their way through the disorganized French lines. They burned and destroyed the siege weapons. They nearly reached the main Christian camp.

After this defeat, Richard ordered an even heavier bombardment of the city. The powerful mangonels hurled their deadly stones against the walls and towers. Some of the stones crashed into the streets of Acre. They burst into fragments and killed anyone standing near the impact.

English archers sent flaming arrows across the walls, setting fire to houses within Acre. The Christians brought their siege towers back to the walls, keeping up a hail of arrows on the defenders scattering below them in the streets.

Acre finally fell after a relentless siege by the crusaders.

Richard still had to breach Acre's thick walls. He ordered sappers to dig underneath the walls. Their task was to remove foundation stones or destroy them with fire or explosives. If the sappers could damage the foundations, the walls would start to fall.

The underground sappers and the artillery fire soon had their intended effect. The Christians breached the walls in several places. Muslims and Christians fought hand to hand over great heaps of rubble where the towers had crashed to the ground.

The Muslim commander sent his men to defend the breaches. This eventually proved a hopeless task. At several points, Christian knights and soldiers dashed into the streets of the city. They spread mayhem wherever they went. They killed hundreds of Muslim soldiers and civilians before they were forced back across the walls.

THE FALL OF ACRE

On the night of July 5, the Maledicta tower, an important strongpoint in the defenses of Acre, crashed to the ground. An immense pile of rubble, easy to defend, now lay in the path. The English king rushed up to the ruins of the tower with his men. He ordered them to remove the debris and clear a way into the city.

Several all-out assaults over the next few days failed. Richard commanded his men to keep trying. He offered gold coins to anyone who could haul away the heavy stones blocking his path into Acre.

Seeing the dire situation of the city, Saladin then ordered an attack on the Christian camp. But the Christians easily drove the attackers back. Richard and his men could sense a victory coming.

The morale of the Muslim troops sank lower. Many of Saladin's men refused to risk their lives in attacks on the Christians. The commanders of Acre, seeing the hopelessness of their situation, sent messengers to Saladin. They asked permission to surrender the city and ask for peace terms from Richard.

Saladin refused their request. If Acre fell to the Christians, then the English king and his men would control the most important stronghold on the coast. They could use this fortress as a base for an attack on Jerusalem. They controlled the sea and could reinforce Acre for as long as necessary.

But Saladin's army could not lift the siege. On July 12, the commanders of Acre finally surrendered. The Christians took the Muslim soldiers prisoner. In just one month, Richard had succeeded where his Christian rivals had been failing for the past two years.

The two sides agreed on a truce. The Muslims would turn over a piece of the True Cross, said to be the cross on which Jesus was crucified. They had captured this holy relic at the Battle of Hattin. The Muslims also agreed to release all Christians taken prisoner. They would surrender the treasury of Acre and pay a ransom for Muslim prisoners held by the Christians.

The Christian commanders entered the city, claiming the finest houses for their headquarters, and taking Muslim commanders hostage for the payment of ransom.

The conquest of Acre was Richard's finest victory yet. He took great pride in his achievement. He wanted it known to one and all that the conquest of Acre was his conquest. French and German soldiers had taken part, but the English king alone had triumphed. When Richard found that Leopold of Austria had planted his flag on the city walls, as if to claim the victory, he angrily ordered it to be hauled down.

English soldiers rushed to Leopold's banner. They took it down from the wall and threw it into a ditch. When he heard the news of what Richard had done, Leopold grew furious. The Austrian duke would never forgive or forget the insult.

DEALING WITH PRISONERS

Before he could bring his army to Jerusalem, Richard had a difficult problem to solve. Because the Muslims had surrendered Acre, several thousand enemy soldiers had survived the siege. They were now being held prisoner in the Christian camp.

The Muslim commanders had agreed to ransom these men when they surrendered. Richard gave Saladin thirty days to meet the ransom demand. In the meantime, the Muslim prisoners had to be kept alive with food and water from the Christian stores.

Bitter at the loss of Acre, Saladin delayed payment of the ransom. He claimed that he had not given the city's commanders permission to surrender. For him, the fight for Acre had not yet ended.

Richard felt anxious to move his army south for an assault on Jerusalem. He became angry and impatient. While his men acted as prison guards, time was wasting at Acre. Saladin, Richard believed, was purposely delaying his ransom payment. The Muslims were using the delay to call up reinforcements and weapons for the defense of Jerusalem.

A month went by with no ransom payment. Finally, on August 20, Richard ended his wait. He rode out from Acre with a company of knights. They brought the Muslim prisoners, bound with ropes, into the plain before Acre.

The helpless prisoners stumbled between lines of Christian soldiers. Under Richard's orders, the soldiers cut the prisoners down with swords and axes. Except for a few high-ranking officers, every single Muslim prisoner was killed without mercy.

Enraged by Richard's actions, Saladin ordered his own troops to murder their Christian prisoners. The killing went on for several days. Thousands of prisoners, bound with ropes and chains, died helplessly.

The massacre at Acre terrified Muslims and Christians alike. Both sides promised vengeance against the other. All expected that this Crusade for the Holy Land and Jerusalem would be the most terrible one yet.

PHILIP QUITS THE HOLY LAND

For King Philip, the fall of Acre was a triumph as well as a helpful excuse. He had grown intensely jealous of Richard. He saw no glory for himself in staying in Palestine. Philip knew he could not match Richard's skill as a general, and that the Angevin ruler would win all the honors and glory of the battles to come.

Philip also saw an advantage in returning to France while Richard was away from home. Richard was protected by the Truce of God. But Philip would have the advantage while the English king remained in the Holy Land. The French could win allies and assemble a powerful army. If anything happened to the English king, the Angevin realm would be at the mercy of France.

Philip sent messengers to Richard's headquarters. The messengers brought the news that the French king was ill. He would be quitting the Crusade immediately and returning to Europe.

The news angered Richard. In his eyes, there was no cause more worthy than the Crusade. To Richard, Philip was a coward and a quitter whose true goal was the overthrow of the Angevin empire.

But Richard accepted Philip's excuse of illness. He didn't try to stop the French king from leaving Acre with his army and fleet. With Philip out of the way, Richard realized, he would be the sole, uncontested commander of the Christian army. The glory of the capture of Jerusalem would be his alone.

THE HOLY

To Muslims, Jerusalem is also a holy city. Muslim armies first captured the city in 637. According to Islam, the prophet Muhammad ascended to heaven from Jerusalem.

In the seventh century, craftsmen from the Byzantine Empire raised a shrine at this site. The shrine is known as the Dome of the Rock. In the center of the shrine is a bare rock. It was from this rock, according to Islamic tradition, that Muhammad made his ascent into heaven.

The Dome of the Rock survives to this day. Its golden dome rises above the historic center of the city. Christians and Jews know this place as the Temple Mount, while Muslims call it the Noble Sanctuary.

In Arabic, Jerusalem was Al Kuds, or The Holy. Only the cities of Mecca and Medina, which were home to Muhammad, were (and are) considered more sacred than Al Kuds.

Philip rode out from Acre to the fortress of Tyre, to the north. With him rode Conrad of Montferrat, the claimant to the throne of Jerusalem. Conrad had allied himself with Philip. He had no intention of helping Richard in his campaign against the holy city.

Conrad would watch and wait. If the city fell, he would be heir to the kingdom of Jerusalem, after Guy of Lusignan. Three days after arriving in Tyre, Philip sailed for home, putting the duke of Burgundy in command of the French forces that stayed with Richard.

PREPARING THE DRIVE ON JERUSALEM

Under Richard's orders, the Christians repaired the walls of Acre. Joanna, Berengaria, and the captive daughter of Isaac Comnenus, the dethroned ruler of Cyprus, remained in the city's palace.

The Christian army gathered its horses, weapons, and food. They loaded the supplies onto a long baggage train, made up of wooden carts drawn by strong horses and mules.

The Muslim army did not remain idle. The Turkish horsemen staged frequent raids on the Christian camp. During one of these raids, Richard personally led a counterattack. In a small company of Hungarian knights, he rode furiously after the retreating Turks.

In a very short time, he was well distant from his own camp and several miles into enemy territory. The Turks wheeled and charged the Hungarians. They took several of the Hungarians, as well as Richard's vassal Hugh of Poitou, captive. Richard galloped against the Turks but did not have the speed to reach them or recover their prisoners.

In the last week of August 1191, the Christians headed south, along the coast road. Richard's goal was to capture the main coastal cities and use them as a base for a drive on Jerusalem. The city lay about fifty miles inland in a region of heavily forested hills.

The fall of Acre was an important victory but only the start of the Crusade. Richard's goal was to take Jerusalem and establish a strong Christian kingdom in this land. It would be this achievement, he believed, that would make his permanent mark on history.

THE MARCH TO JERUSALEM

RICHARD HAD CAPTURED THE STRONGHOLD OF Acre in the summer of 1191. He then prepared for a march to Jerusalem. He meant to capture the holy city from the Muslims.

His plan was to lead his army eighty miles south to the port of Jaffa. He would fortify this place by raising strong stone walls. He would then use Jaffa as a base for his conquest of the holy city.

The siege of Acre had lasted two years. Many men had died from battle, from hunger, and from disease. Those who survived now had a chance to rest. They enjoyed the delights of the city. They had comfortable beds, secure homes to live in, and plentiful food in the markets.

The summer wore on as Richard made ready. The army gathered a baggage train. It included hundreds of wagons, pulled by strong mules. The soldiers collected enough food and water to last for several weeks. Finally, the march from Acre began on August 22, 1191.

Richard led his army along the coast road. The English marched in front. Burgundians and Flemish soldiers followed. The knights of the Templars and Hospitallers made up a strong cavalry force. The French, under the duke of Burgundy, brought up the rear.

By taking this route, Richard avoided battle with Saladin. The English king knew the Muslims controlled the roads inland that led to Jerusalem. He did not want to fight yet. He would avoid battle and spare his men until he arrived at his goal.

Richard had another good reason for keeping near the sea. The ships following Richard's army south could provide supplies and reinforcements. The sailors could come ashore and fight, if Saladin attacked. If necessary, the crusaders could retreat to the ships.

AMBUSHES IN THE HILLS

The crusaders passed through the wooded highlands of Mount Carmel. This was a place of thick oak and pine groves, steep foothills, and well-hidden caves. It was a perfect spot for surprise attacks.

Saladin followed the crusader army and camped a few miles away. The crusaders trudged over the hills on narrow trails. The Muslims staged ambushes along the way. They showered the Christians with arrows and bombarded them with rolling rocks. They attacked out of nowhere, wielding knives, arrows, and spears.

The hot weather made the heavily armored Christian soldiers miserable. By day, they battled the Muslims on the

KNIGHTLY ORDERS ON CRUSADE

The Crusades inspired the creation of two important orders of knights, the Templars and the Hospitallers. Two French knights, Hughes de Payens and Godfrey de Saint Omer, formed the Templars in 1118. The members of this order were monks as well as soldiers. Their symbol was a red cross on a white background. They built a headquarters on the Temple Mount, an important holy site in Jerusalem. The Templars vowed to protect pilgrims arriving in the Holy Land from Europe. They fought in several key battles during the Crusades.

Gerard Thom, or the Blessed Gerard, founded the order of the Hospitallers around 1100. This order owned hostels and took in sick and injured pilgrims in the Holy Land. They grew into a powerful army of knights, sworn to fight alongside crusaders from Europe. Their symbol was a white cross on a black background.

The Templars and the Hospitallers fought alongside Richard I in Palestine. Some returned to Europe after his crusade, while others remained in the Holy Land. As an independent and wealthy army, the Templars posed a threat to established kings in Europe. A French king, Philip IV, destroyed the Templars in 1307. He had them arrested and ordered many of them to be burned at the stake.

The Hospitallers had a better fate. After the fall of Acre, the last crusader stronghold, they moved to the island of Rhodes, in the Aegean Sea, in 1291. Later they occupied the island of Malta, off the coast of Sicily in the Mediterranean Sea. As rent, they paid one Maltese falcon every year to the king of Sicily, their overlord. The Hospitallers survive to this day as the Order of Malta.

trails. At night, the men froze in a sharp cold. They had to fight stinging spiders that invaded their tents and clothes.

Richard marched his men in the morning. He allowed them to rest in the afternoon. Every other day, he called a halt. It was a hard, exhausting march.

The crusaders labored forward in their heavy armor, struggling to carry their iron weapons. Behind them trailed their long baggage train, their catapults, and their unruly herds of horses.

South of Mount Carmel, the level coast road followed the sea. The march was easier, but the ambushes continued. The Arabs followed Richard's army and attacked from the rear and the flanks. They murdered stragglers without mercy. They meant to avenge the massacre of Muslim prisoners before the walls of Acre.

Richard led counterattacks against the Arab raiders. He drove them away wherever he met them. His fighting ability was well known to the Muslims. Few of them dared a combat against him.

The Christians also put their crossbows to good use. These weapons fired a deadly bolt at long range. The crossbowmen used them to kill and drive away the enemy raiders.

Richard had instilled great discipline in his army. He kept the army in formation even as it came under constant ambush. One Arab witness, Baha al-Din, reported:

> The enemy moved in order of battle: their infantry marched between us and their cavalry, keeping as level and firm as a wall. Each foot-soldier had a thick cassock of felt and under it a mail-shirt so strong

that our arrows made no impression on them. They, meanwhile, shot at us with crossbows which struck down horse and man among the Muslims. I noted among them men who had from one to ten shafts sticking in their backs, yet trudged on at their ordinary pace and did not fall out of their ranks.[1]

Richard avoided a direct battle and pressed his army to reach its goal. He knew that the longer the Christians took, the longer the Muslim defenders of Jerusalem would have to prepare their city for the attack.

The Christians reached the ancient Roman port of Caesarea, south of Mount Carmel, in early September. They took rest from the dangers they had faced along the way.

THE BATTLE OF ARSOUF

Saladin followed the Christian army south. He led a powerful force, made up of archers and skilled horsemen. Most of the men were either Turks or Kurds. There were also Mamluks (Egyptian slaves) and mercenaries. Some of the mercenaries were Europeans, fighting only for pay and booty.

The Muslim Turks were expert in the use of bow and arrow. Their bows were about a yard long, made of horn and sinew. Their arrows could fly farther than those of the Christians. They could penetrate body armor and kill instantly. Fighting hand to hand, the Muslims used javelins, daggers, and swords.

Saladin followed the Christians south to Arsouf. A broad plain spread out north from the small port city.

Saladin believed this to be a perfect time and place for a pitched battle. The Christians had lost hundreds of men to his ambushes. Saladin believed they were growing weary on this long, hot march.

The thick forests would disguise his men until they were almost upon the Christians. On the coastal plain, the Muslim horsemen would have room to maneuver and charge. Saladin intended to cut off Richard's retreat to the north and south and drive his army into the sea.

Richard knew a battle was coming. He wanted to give his army time to prepare. He sent messengers to Saladin asking for a truce and a parley.

Saladin sent his brother, Saif al-Din (or Safadin), to talk with the English king. Richard greeted the man politely. But the king was ready for battle. He did not want to make any agreement with the Muslims. He demanded that Saladin give up all of Palestine to the Christians. The demand ended the parley immediately, as Richard knew it would. Both sides prepared for battle.

Early in the morning of September 7, Richard ordered his men into place. His army lined up, facing the plain to the east. He sent the baggage train to the coast, in the rear. The crossbowmen marched to the front, with the mounted knights waiting in the middle.

The Knights Templars made up the right wing of Richard's army. The king commanded the Norman and English troops in the center. On the left stood the French under the duke of Burgundy, and the Knights Hospitallers.

The Muslims began their attack in mid-morning. Foot soldiers rushed forward, hurling spears and arrows at the

Christian lines. Then a group of Muslim cavalry passed the infantry and charged the French and Hospitallers on Richard's left flank.

Saladin's plan was to throw this portion of Richard's army into retreat. He knew the French and the Hospitallers made up the weak spot in Richard's line. He would then roll up the line, from north to south.

Watching the Muslim attack, and guessing Saladin's plan, Richard ordered his men to hold their fire. He knew the first wave of arrows would be the most effective. His impatient knights begged him to charge the Muslims. But he refused, holding fast and waiting for the right moment.

The Christians stood in place while the Muslims charged their lines. Saladin's skirmishers dashed into the crusaders, wielding their swords. A violent clash took place, and a few men fell to the ground. The Muslims retreated, and the crusaders formed up their line again.

Finally, the Templars on the right flank could hold back no longer. In defiance of Richard's orders, they charged out against the Muslims. The knights galloped past the crossbowmen and dashed into the open plain. They made straight for the Muslim horsemen. Seeing he could do nothing to hold them back, Richard charged with them, leading in the center.

The Muslims watched in terror as thousands of heavily armored, screaming men made directly for them, lances and swords glinting in the broiling midday sun. Just before the impact, the Muslim foot soldiers began throwing down their weapons and fleeing back to the forests surrounding Arsouf.

The battlefield fell into noisy chaos. Richard's knights clashed with the enemy horsemen, raising clouds of dust and toppling wounded and dead men from their mounts.

The Muslims soon broke and fled the field. Saladin rallied some of his men for a counterattack. But the Christians were too strong and eager for the victory. Saladin had to call a retreat and leave the plain of Arsouf in Richard's hands.

A HARD DECISION AT RAMLEH

Richard had won another victory at Arsouf. While the Muslims retreated, he wasted no time. He meant to press on to Jerusalem as soon as possible. He ordered his men to bury their dead. He re-formed the army for the march. Then he led the Christians south again.

In a short time, the crusaders reached Jaffa. The Muslims had captured this stronghold after the fall of Jerusalem. They had destroyed its walls and then retreated. Richard called a halt. He ordered his men to repair and strengthen the walls of Jaffa.

He again sent envoys to Saladin to discuss peace terms. He demanded the return of Jerusalem and all the land west of the Jordan River. Saladin refused this demand. Jerusalem was a holy city to Muslims as well as Christians. Saladin felt it was his duty to hold it.

Saladin believed Jerusalem could defend itself. The city had strong walls. Towers rose over its gates. A large garrison of soldiers and officers lived within the city.

Richard knew a siege of Jerusalem would be difficult. He decided to make a bold proposal. He suggested that Saladin concede all of Palestine to Saladin's brother, Safadin. His brother should then marry Richard's sister, Joanna.

As queen of the Holy Land, Joanna would control the coastal cities that Richard had conquered. Jerusalem would become a city open to Muslims as well as Christians. Both sides would release all prisoners, and the Muslims would restore the True Cross to the Christians.

As a feudal king, Richard was used to making alliances through marriage. But Saladin thought the offer a joke or a trick. He didn't respond to the offer immediately. He told his brother of Richard's plan.

Richard proposed to Safadin that he convert to Christianity. He would win the sister of the most powerful man in Europe and the title to all of Palestine. But Safadin refused to give up Islam. Joanna, when she heard of the plan, reacted with horror. She absolutely refused to marry a Muslim, no matter how much land she would gain as her wedding present.

Richard dropped his bold plan for a peace agreement. He reinforced and rested his army. In the middle of November, he led the Christians to the town of Ramleh, along the road from Jaffa to Jerusalem. There he stopped. He sent scouts and spies forward to Jerusalem.

The scouts entered the city in disguise. They moved about the streets and markets. They tried to see how many soldiers were defending the city. They watched the towers and walls. When the time was right, they returned to the Christian camp to make their reports.

Jerusalem was a strong, well-fortified city. An entire army of Muslim archers and infantry lived within its walls. It was also winter—a bad time for a campaign. The weather was cold and rainy, making it difficult to maneuver.

Richard scouted the Muslim defenses and waited for the right moment to strike. The winter began, bringing cold, dampness, and heavy rains to the hills surrounding the holy city.

Many of Richard's men, bored and idle at Ramleh and Jaffa, grew discouraged. The conditions in their camp were growing worse by the day. Many soldiers were dying of disease. Food supplies were low and the army was going hungry. Worse, the harassment from Arab and Turkish raiders continued.

The sight of Jerusalem did not raise the army's spirits. The men could now see how difficult it would be to capture and hold the city. The glorious idea of retaking Jerusalem faded in plain view of the harsh reality. The walls were high and strong. The Muslim army was rested and ready to defend them.

The knights of the Templars and Hospitallers gave Richard some advice. They warned him that Saladin had brought reinforcements from Egypt. The Christians were now outnumbered. If they defeated Saladin's army, they would then have to fight his allies from Egypt. And, in the words of historian Steven Runciman: " . . . if he captured Jerusalem, they added, what then? The visiting Crusaders when they had paid their pilgrimage would all return home to Europe; and the native soldiery was not numerous enough to hold it against the forces of united Islam."[2]

Richard had to consider this advice. His great dream had long been to recapture Jerusalem and return it to Christian rule. But once inside the city, it would be very difficult to defend it. Surrounded by Saladin's armies, the city could not hold out, at least not without his leadership. He would have to remain in Jerusalem indefinitely.

If the Christians stayed in their camp at Ramleh, the Muslims would cut off their supply line to the coast. The idle army of Europeans would gradually starve.

The Lionheart looked out at the distant walls of Jerusalem from Ramleh. He made one of the hardest decisions of his life. He halted the advance on the city. He waited six weeks and then turned back to the coast. Jerusalem still belonged to Saladin and the Muslims.

FIGHTING AT ASCALON

In January 1192, the crusader army marched from Ramleh back to the seacoast. Many of the men now lost heart, as well as their faith in the king's leadership. The duke of Burgundy and the entire French army deserted Richard. They retreated to Acre and Tyre, where Conrad of Montferrat was plotting against Richard.

At Ascalon, the crusaders who stayed with the king found a ruined city. Several years earlier, Saladin had destroyed the walls and the houses, leaving only rubble and stones behind. In miserable cold and stormy weather, the hungry crusaders raised makeshift shelters in the ruins.

Richard saw that his army was in danger of turning into a starving, desperate mob. To keep his men busy, he ordered them to rebuild the walls of Ascalon. He also sent messengers to Acre, asking the French soldiers to return to the Crusade.

They agreed, on condition that they would be free to return to Europe after Easter. Richard would also be responsible for paying and feeding the men. The French arrived at Ascalon. But within a month, Richard had no money to pay them. The French quit Richard's army once again.

Richard army was growing smaller. Leopold of Austria was already angry with Richard. His army in Ascalon was doing nothing. He complained about the hard work of raising the walls. He quit the city and the Holy Land. He returned to Austria, now Richard's sworn enemy.

Leopold's true reason may have been envy and hatred of Richard. Leopold would never forget the humiliation he had suffered at Acre, when the English soldiers had thrown his banners down from the city walls.

As the weather grew warmer, and Ascalon revived, the army's spirits rose. Richard led raiding parties out from inside the walls, capturing enemy caravans and taking Muslim prisoners. On Easter Sunday, 1192, the king organized a feast for his men.

THE DEATH OF A CRUSADER

His long absence from England was causing Richard serious problems back home. Richard's younger brother, John, was causing trouble. He did not feel satisfied with the many castles and estates Richard had granted to him. John had agreed to keep the peace. But by the spring of 1192, he was fighting against Richard's officials and trying to seize the throne.

When messengers from England brought the news, Richard realized he was in danger of losing the entire Angevin realm. He prepared to leave Palestine. He would appoint a new leader to carry on the Crusade in his place.

Guy de Lusignan was Richard's own vassal. But the king knew that Conrad of Montferrat commanded much more respect as a general than did Lusignan. He sent for Conrad, and the duke of Burgundy, to join the crusaders at Ascalon.

Richard announced that he would accept Conrad as the king of Jerusalem. Conrad would become the ruler of all the Christians in the Holy Land.

Richard then sold the island of Cyprus to Guy de Lusignan. The price was forty thousand bezants. Guy sought the help of Italian merchants to buy Cyprus. They were eager to loan him the money. They wanted to use Cyprus as a base for trade in the eastern Mediterranean.

For Richard, the island was a reward for Guy de Lusignan's cooperation. Guy's brother, Aimery, established the Lusignan dynasty. For the next three centuries, the Lusignans would rule Cyprus.

Shortly after Easter, when he heard the news that Richard had accepted him as the king of Jerusalem, Conrad of Montferrat sank to his knees in happiness and gratitude. In an instant, his hopes and dreams had come true—or so he believed.

Conrad had made many enemies while ruling the city of Tyre. The most dangerous of them was the "Old Man of the Mountain." He was a leader of the Muslim sect of Hashashim, or Assassins.

These trained killers lived in the mountains near the city, in a place impossible to capture. They practiced strange rites and performed whirling, frenzied dances. Under the Old Man's orders, they sometimes went out on suicidal missions of murder. The Old Man's teachings convinced them that, after their deaths, they would gain entry to a paradise of well-watered, lush gardens.

Conrad angered the Old Man by not punishing the murder of several Hashashim in the city of Tyre. Yet he paid little heed to the rumors that the Hashashim were plotting his death. He often went out into the streets without escort or guard.

On the evening of April 28, 1192, Conrad was walking alone in Tyre. At one dark street corner, he was met by two men disguised as Christian monks. The men stopped him and held out a letter, claiming that the message was for him.

Conrad did not suspect any trouble. When he reached for the letter, the men pulled out daggers. They plunged the daggers into Conrad's body. The king of Jerusalem died on the spot.

The murder of Conrad caused an uproar in Tyre and the Holy Land. The news spread quickly to Europe. Many people believed that Richard was behind the assassination. Conrad and Richard had long been rivals. Conrad's retreat from the crusade, everyone believed, had deeply angered the English king.

According to these rumors, Richard had no intention of allowing Conrad to rule in Jerusalem or anyplace else. Killing Conrad was simply the easiest way to bring his own ally, Guy de Lusignan, to the throne.

Philip of France, hearing the news of Conrad's murder, believed these rumors. He accused Richard to all who would listen. The murder of Conrad of Montferrat blackened Richard's reputation. Many European rulers, including Philip, had much to gain by cutting Richard down to size.

ANOTHER CAMPAIGN FOR JERUSALEM

After the death of Conrad, and the sale of Cyprus to Guy de Lusignan, there were no claimants to the throne of Jerusalem. Richard quickly arranged for his nephew, Henry of Champagne, to marry Conrad's widow, Isabella, who was now in control of Tyre.

By this action, Henry became the uncontested king of Jerusalem. He immediately gathered an army and set out to join Richard at Ascalon.

In the meantime, Richard left Ascalon and marched down the coast road toward Egypt. With a small company of well-armed knights, he reached the Muslim-held fortress of Darum. On the beaches near the citadel, he assembled siege towers and engines.

Richard began bombarding the walls of Darum with heavy stones. Engineers crept underneath the walls to undermine them. In just four days, the Muslim garrison asked for surrender terms.

Richard refused their plea for a truce. He demanded they come out of Darum and fight. In the battle that followed, the Christians took several hundred prisoners and killed dozens of the best Muslim fighters. Richard left a garrison at Darum, gathered his prisoners, and returned to Ascalon.

As spring turned to summer in 1192, Richard took advantage of fair weather to mount one last drive on Jerusalem. He called on the duke of Burgundy to march south from Acre. While Saladin again fortified his defenses, the crusaders marched to Beit Nuba, on the outskirts of Jerusalem.

Richard waited impatiently for his reinforcements. At the same time, Saladin ordered his own supplies and reinforcements to Jerusalem from Egypt. When a supply train from Egypt approached through the hills, Richard led a small force to capture it.

Outnumbered by four to one, the Christians overcame the enemy defenders. They captured the supply train, which included horses, weapons, food, gold, and silks.

Shortly after this victory, Henry of Champagne arrived at Beit Nuba with his reinforcements. But the Christian camp was still sharply divided, with French and English soldiers often fighting in the open over their privileges and the spoils of war. Finally, as Richard put off the decision to attack Jerusalem, the French once again deserted the crusader army.

A HEROIC FIGHT AT JAFFA

Richard called his last retreat. The crusaders marched to Jaffa, then north to Acre. Hearing the news that Richard had moved away from his base at Jaffa, Saladin led his army to the coast.

After four days, and with their commander Richard absent, the fifty men surviving within the walls of Jaffa raised a flag of truce. They agreed to surrender the city, if they were not relieved by the following afternoon.

The Muslims waited, confident that nothing could save the garrison at Jaffa. But they were proved wrong. Hearing of the siege, Richard had set out immediately by galleys from the port at Acre. Several ships were separated from the fleet during the voyage. By the time he reached Jaffa, he had only three galleys. He came ashore at dawn, with only a few hours left in the truce.

With Richard approaching by sea, Saladin ordered an immediate attack on Jaffa. The Muslims demanded that the garrison surrender. The Christians agreed and began to leave the town by its main gate. But even as they were laying down their weapons, scouts spotted Richard's tiny fleet reaching the shore.

Terrified by the sudden appearance of the king of England, the Muslims immediately took to their heels. Richard walked ashore, ready for a fight. He quickly raised fortifications along the beach and entered Jaffa, planting his banner on the city walls. He ordered his soldiers to repair the damaged walls and pitched his own tent outside the city, daring the Muslims to attack.

That night, spies brought word to Saladin that Richard was sleeping, almost unprotected, in a royal tent at the foot of the Jaffa wall. Not believing his good luck, Saladin ordered his men to assault the city and capture the king. The Muslims approached under cover of darkness. A guard in the Christian camp heard their approach.

The calls woke Richard, who instantly assembled his knights and companions for the fight. He led his men into Jaffa, where they routed the Muslims. The force of only a few dozen knights then rode outside the walls, swords at the ready. Richard assembled two lines of foot soldiers and crossbowmen to face Saladin's charging cavalry.

Muslim horsemen charged the Christian lines for hours. Richard shouted encouragement to his men and gathered his knights for counterattacks. The two sides fought desperately. The commanders threatened their men with instant execution if they tried to flee.

Eventually, Saladin called off the charges. While the Muslims regrouped, Richard rode out alone, waving his sword and taunting the enemy as cowards. He challenged the Muslim horsemen to single combat, man-to-man, in order to decide the battle. Nobody accepted the challenge.

The courage of Richard at the battle of Jaffa was recorded by one chronicler as follows:

> The king was a giant in the battle and everywhere in
> the field, now here, now there, wherever the attacks

of the Turks raged most fiercely. On that day his sword shone like lightning and many of the Turks felt its edge. Some were cloven in two from their helmet to their teeth; others lost their heads, arms and other limbs, lopped off at a single blow.[3]

Richard had scored an incredible victory at Jaffa. But the many hard battles and the campaign for Jerusalem left both sides exhausted. Christian and Muslim envoys met to hammer out an agreement.

They agreed on a truce to last three years. The Christians surrendered Ascalon but kept Tyre, Acre, and several other coastal cities. Christians would also have the right to make the pilgrimage to Jerusalem. But the holy city remained under Muslim control.

The Third Crusade had ended. Richard had fought bravely for the Christian side but had not attained his goal. His worst enemy had turned out to be men professing the Christian faith. The king of France and others had abandoned the Crusade, while Conrad of Montferrat and others schemed only for their own power and glory.

Not even Richard's forceful leadership of men on the battlefield could overcome these bitter divisions. Now he would return to his homeland. He would resume the endless struggle for power and privilege in feudal Europe.

RETREAT FROM THE HOLY LAND

IN OCTOBER 1192, RICHARD GAVE UP THE campaign for Jerusalem. He sailed away from the Holy Land. His sister, Joanna, and his wife, Berengaria, left with him.

He was in a hurry. Messengers had brought him some bad news from England. Prince John, his brother, was gathering his own army. John was capturing castles and claiming royal power. If Richard did not get home quickly, he might lose his throne.

Sailing all the way to England in the winter would take months. But Richard knew he could not pass through France. King Philip was hostile toward him. Philip had already attacked Angevin lands in Normandy.

If Richard crossed France, he would be taking a big risk. If the French met him on the way, they would delay him. They would try to kill him or take him prisoner.

Emperor Henry VI was also Richard's enemy. He ruled many different states in central Europe. He sent messages to his vassals, including Duke Leopold of Austria. If they were to spot Richard, they were to capture him and turn him over to Henry.

A FATEFUL DECISION

Richard turned his fleet up the Adriatic Sea. He knew sentries were watching for his ship. He ordered his ship to sail past the Italian port of Brindisi. He wanted his enemies to think he meant to land close by.

But then he turned away. He sailed south and then west, to the coast of Sicily. He considered what to do next.

Winter was approaching, and voyaging by sea was dangerous. Pirates sailed these waters. He had to land somewhere, and soon.

To sail back to England was impossible. He would have to pass the Strait of Gibraltar, between Spain and North Africa. But strong currents and heavy winds blew to the east. His ships would never be able to pass the strait.

He could not land in Spain or France. The nobles who controlled these coasts were allied to the count of Toulouse, his enemy. He could not land in southern Italy. He would be recognized and turned over to Henry VI, who had many loyal vassals in the region.

He returned to the Adriatic, hugging the coast of Dalmatia on the eastern side. He would land in disguise on the northern coast of Italy. With a small company, he would make his way overland through Austria, Germany, and Moravia. He meant to reach the lands of Henry the

Lion, his ally in Saxony. He would reach the North Sea and take a ship for England.

Richard landed on the coast of Istria, at the northern limits of the Adriatic Sea. He had disguised himself as a pilgrim. He believed that no one would interfere with him.

THE CAPTURE OF THE KING

The king's company reached the town of Erdburg, outside Vienna. They took rooms in a small inn. In the meantime, rumors were spreading of his secret march. Many people believed that Richard was passing through the lands of the German emperor, Henry VI. Leopold, the duke of Austria, sent his sentries into the countryside to search for him.

The people of Erdburg listened carefully to the foreign pilgrims, who spoke German with a strange foreign accent. They also heard Richard's men speak to him with respect, as if he were a very important person. This was not typical behavior for pilgrims. The people suspected a deception.

Feeling unwell, Richard took to his bed at the inn. He sent a young boy to a market for food. The boy attracted suspicion with his proud bearing, as if he belonged to a royal court. He carried strange silver coins from Syria, a land near Palestine. One day, he also wore ornate gloves that could only belong to an important noble—or a king.

The news reached Leopold's sentries. They came to the market and arrested the boy. They threatened him and may have tortured him. Finally, the boy revealed Richard's hiding place at the inn.

Leopold's soldiers rushed to the inn. They surrounded it and prepared to search the building. Hearing a commotion outside, Richard disguised himself as a kitchen servant. He rushed downstairs and began working in front of the fire.

The soldiers burst into the inn. After searching the rooms, they came into the kitchen. One of them was a veteran of the siege of Acre. He recognized Richard immediately. The king was arrested.[1]

A sentry brought news of the arrest to Leopold, who then sent messengers to Henry. The German emperor quickly sent word of the capture to his ally, King Philip of France: ". . . our dearly beloved cousin, Leopold, Duke of Austria, captured the king . . . in an humble house in a village in the vicinity of Vienna. Inasmuch as he is now in our power, and has always done his utmost for your annoyance and disturbance, what we have above stated we have thought proper to notify to your nobleness, knowing that the same is well pleasing to [you]. . . ."[2]

Henry ordered Leopold to bring Richard to the castle of Dürnstein. The gloomy stronghold perched high on a cliff along the banks of the Danube River. Guards kept watch on the king within the castle. They gave him food and water, but did not allow him to communicate with anyone.

Richard did not lose heart. He kept up his mood by playing practical jokes on the guards. He offered to wrestle them and, sometimes, plied them with wine to make them drunk and foolish. Many visitors came to see him, and vassals came to do homage. One chronicler, Ralph of

Coggeshall, wrote that "no tribulation could cloud the countenance of this most serene prince. . . . His words remained cheerful and jocund, his actions fierce or most courageous as time, place, reason or person demanded."[3]

Richard did not intend to stay long in Germany, however. He spent the cold winter months plotting his freedom and return to England.

KING PHILIP

King Philip of France saw this as his chance to destroy Richard once and for all. He offered an alliance to Prince John. If Richard stayed in prison, John could declare himself the new king of England. He could then make a permanent peace with France.

To seal the alliance, Philip asked John to marry Alais. Ever since the death of Henry II, Alais had been under guard in Rouen, the capital of Normandy.

John agreed to this arrangement, even though he was already married to Isabelle of Gloucester. He promised to push Isabelle aside and take the hand of Alais. He agreed to permanently surrender lands in Normandy that Philip had conquered. He also agreed to do homage to Philip for the part of Normandy John controlled as the new duke.

In England, the news of Richard's capture reached Eleanor, Richard's mother, and quickly spread through the kingdom. Eleanor wrote to princes and church leaders all over Europe. She asked them to persuade Henry to free Richard.

Eleanor reminded them that Richard had fought valiantly in the Holy Land against the Muslims. He had captured Acre and other important cities for the Christians. Surely Henry had no right to hold such a man prisoner!

Eleanor also wrote to the pope in Rome, asking him to help free Richard. The pope had the power to excommunicate Henry. Through excommunication, the pope expelled people from the church. They could not make confession or attend mass. If they died excommunicated, Christians believed, their souls would burn in hell for eternity.

Soon, many important men from England were traveling to Germany to demand the king's release. They

After being imprisoned at a castle in Dürnstein, Richard was moved to this castle in Trifels, Germany.

tried to send messages to Richard. The king realized he only had to be patient.

Henry knew Richard had many allies. He also knew the king would attempt an escape. He moved Richard from one castle prison to the next, to make sure nobody could be sure where his prisoner was kept.

A SCHEMING PRINCE

Prince John, Richard's younger brother, saw a great opportunity in Henry's capture of the king. If Richard remained in a German prison, John could claim the throne for himself. He would become the new king of England and the lord of Richard's domains on the continent.

John's army began marching around England. The prince seized towns, robbed monasteries, and besieged the castles of lords still loyal to Richard. John sent messages to his mother, Eleanor, claiming that Richard would never return to England. He wanted Eleanor's support for his claim as the king of England.

Not trusting John, Eleanor wouldn't agree. She believed Richard would eventually win his freedom. She ordered the arrest of foreign soldiers fighting for John in England. She also ordered defenses raised in English ports. The defenses would protect the realm against an invasion from the continent. She demanded that the English lords and bishops swear an oath of loyalty to Richard.

Eleanor was playing for time. She knew that Henry could keep Richard a captive for life. If he wanted to, he could also have Richard murdered. Eventually, the king's absence would provoke a civil war. She would be forced to recognize John, who was next in line to the throne, as the new king.

RICHARD WINS HIS FREEDOM

In March 1193, Henry brought Richard to the imperial court in Speyer, Germany. The court met every year at Easter time. The emperor's vassals gathered to resolve their many disputes.

Henry intended to make a decision concerning Richard. He wanted to gain as much as he could from releasing the king. The emperor brought Richard before his assembly of knights, princes, and leaders of the church.

The emperor first rose to speak before his court. He accused Richard of murdering Conrad of Montferrat during the Crusade. He also charged Richard with treason. He said Richard had made a pact with the enemy leader, Saladin. This agreement left Jerusalem under the control of the Muslims.

Richard rose to answer the charges. He spoke for a long time and with much feeling. He told of his adventures in the Holy Land, and how he had defeated the Muslims many times with his own skill and bravery.

Richard convinced Henry's court that he had acted in good faith. It was the cowardice of others, he explained, that had weakened his army. The French king had abandoned the Crusade.

Many other allies had sailed away as well. They had left Richard to fight the Muslims alone. This treachery, and not any pact with Saladin, had ended his quest for the capture of Jerusalem.

William the Breton, the court poet of the French king Philip, was present at the court of Speyer. William described the event: "When Richard replied he spoke so eloquently and regally, in so lion-hearted a manner, that it was as though he had forgotten where he was . . . and imagined himself to be seated on the throne of his ancestors. . . ."[4]

Richard convinced many people in Henry's court that he was sincere. After the speech, Henry immediately dropped his charges. But he still held Richard as his hostage.

The emperor moved Richard from Speyer to the city of Trifels. Guards put Richard in a dungeon. They prevented him from communicating with any of his friends or vassals.

The emperor also demanded a huge ransom of one hundred thousand marks.[5] Richard agreed to raise the money and also to give Henry fifty ships and two hundred knights, for the emperor to use for a year.

Henry allowed Richard to meet with Hubert Walter, his trusted adviser. Richard set Hubert the task of raising the ransom money in England. He also appointed Walter as the chief justiciar of England.

Walter returned to England. His task was to raise a fortune, as quickly as possible. He asked the church and the nobles to contribute. The church leaders raised money by turning over some of their silver and gold.

The people of England also paid a special tax of 25 percent on all the money they earned. In the meantime, Henry sent Richard to a castle prison in Trifels.

A few weeks later, William Longchamp sailed across the English Channel and met with Henry. Only a part of the ransom had been raised. But Longchamp persuaded the emperor to let Richard go. To make sure all the money would be paid, England would turn over hostages.

TROUBLE IN NORMANDY

Richard's capture had given Philip, the king of France, a golden opportunity. Philip had assembled his army and marched into the duchy of Normandy. This land belonged to the Angevin rulers. The French captured many Norman castles and persuaded several lords to swear their loyalty to Philip.

The French king also surrounded the important stronghold of Gisors. Before the siege could begin, he sent an offer of truce to the castellan (commander) of Gisors, Gilbert de Vascoeuil.

Gilbert's job was to protect the castle for Richard. But Richard was still in prison in Germany. For all Gilbert knew, the English king might stay a captive forever. In the meantime, France would grow stronger. The defenses of Gisors would wear down as the French occupied Normandy. Philip easily persuaded Gilbert to open the gates and surrender Gisors without a fight.

Philip then marched to Rouen, the capital of Normandy. His sister Alais was still held prisoner in the city, on the orders of Eleanor. When he reached the walls of Rouen, Philip announced that Prince John had done homage to him as the new duke of Normandy. Therefore, he claimed, the French had every right to occupy the city.

Rouen was a much stronger place than Gisors. The city had thick walls, high towers, and a wide moat. A powerful garrison stood ready to protect the city from a siege. The men of the garrison were Normans, not French. If necessary, they would come out to meet the French army in battle.

Realizing that Rouen would not give up without a fight, Philip had brought several catapults to batter the walls. But the French could not hope to capture Rouen with a siege. The military commander of Rouen, the earl of Leicester, was still loyal to Richard.

The earl was not impressed by Philip's claim that France now controlled Normandy. He refused to cooperate with Philip. But he did open the gates and let down the main drawbridge. If Philip and the armies of France wished to visit Rouen, Leicester announced, they could enter peacefully anytime they wanted.

Philip drew away from the trap. He called off his troops. The citadel of Rouen remained in Norman hands.

RANSOMING THE KING

With the castles and lands he captured in Normandy, Philip was growing richer and stronger. In the meantime,

129

his archenemy Richard was held prisoner. Philip still believed he might be able to capture all of Normandy. His goal was to make Normandy a permanent part of France.

Richard may have felt frustration and despair. It may have seemed the emperor would never release him. In one song that Richard composed, he expressed his feelings:

> My vassals and my barons, English, Normans, Poitevins, and Gascons, are well aware that I had no companion so poor that I would leave him in prison for lack of money. I say this not as a rebuke; but I myself am still a prisoner. Those young knights of Anjou and Touraine who now enjoy both wealth and health know well of my plight far from them in a stranger's hands. They used to love me dearly, but now not a jot. The plains stand empty of splendid arms now that I am a prisoner.[6]

In June 1193, Philip asked to meet with Henry. Philip's plan was to take Richard captive himself. He would throw the English king into a French prison—permanently—and see his ally Prince John crowned as the new king of England.

Messengers brought news of Philip's campaign to Richard. The king realized that he would have to escape his prison as soon as possible. He must also prevent any truce between Henry and Philip.

Richard offered Henry an even bigger ransom of one hundred fifty thousand marks.[7] He also helped Henry to make peace with some rebel lords in Germany. Pleased with these actions, Henry agreed to the new ransom. He would accept a first payment of one hundred thousand marks. England would then send a group of hostages. The emperor would set Richard free and keep the hostages prisoner until the rest of the ransom was paid.

Through the summer and fall, Richard's men continued to raise money. Richard's subjects in England, Normandy, Anjou, and Aquitaine paid heavy taxes and fees to the king's representatives.

Henry felt satisfied that Richard could raise the money. The emperor announced that he would release the king early in the next year. But Philip and John, Richard's brother, were also raising money. They were determined to keep Richard a prisoner, one way or the other. They offered to buy Richard from Henry for the sum of one hundred fifty thousand marks.

Henry called another meeting of his princes. Many of them had made agreements and alliances with Richard over the past year. They respected Richard's crusade in the Holy Land. They did not approve of Henry's capture of a Christian king who had fought the Muslims.

These princes and dukes asked the emperor to let Richard go. Henry thought it over, then made one last demand. Richard must surrender England to him. He could remain king as the emperor's vassal. But if he wanted to remain king of England, he would have to pay Henry a tithe of five thousand English pounds a year.[8]

Richard agreed to the new terms. He turned over the first payment of one hundred thousand marks and the hostages. On February 4, 1194, in the city of Mainz, Henry finally released him. According to legend, when the news reached King Philip, he exclaimed, "Look to yourself, the devil is loose!"[9]

Richard sailed down the Rhine River in a fleet of small boats. During his journey, he made alliances with many of the lords in the region. His goal was to form a coalition against the French king.

After a journey of several weeks, Richard finally reached Antwerp, near the English Channel. He intended to cross the Channel as quickly as possible, to end any chance Henry had of recapturing him. He still didn't trust Henry. He knew he was still valuable to the emperor as a prisoner.

In the meantime, Henry had changed his mind about releasing Richard. The English king was worth too much to him. Henry sent a company of knights to recapture the king. But when the knights reached Antwerp, Richard was nowhere to be found.

On March 13, Richard had reached the English port of Sandwich. He had been away from England, on Crusade and in German dungeons, for nearly four years.

THE LAST
CAMPAIGNS IN
FRANCE

AFTER RICHARD GAINED HIS FREEDOM, HE sailed to the English port of Sandwich. He rode to the cathedral of Canterbury, the holiest Christian shrine of the realm. There, at the tomb of Thomas Becket, he gave thanks for his release.

Richard then journeyed back to London. Riding in a grand procession of knights and courtiers, he greeted thousands of people who lined the streets to cheer his return.

After his return to England, Richard immediately sent messengers to the court of King Philip of France. He demanded that the French king give up all of the Angevin lands he had occupied during Richard's captivity.

Richard found that the huge ransom paid for his release had emptied the English treasury. Richard also found

England suffering from the raids of mercenaries, raised by his brother John. While Richard had been locked away in Germany, John had been plotting against him.

Seeking the crown for himself, John had raised these mercenary bands to stir up trouble and help him usurp Richard's throne. John had captured Nottingham Castle, an important stronghold. Soon after his procession into London, Richard assembled another army. He led this army to Nottingham.

A RETURN TO POWER

The king reached the walls of Nottingham Castle on March 24, 1194. A group of rebellious lords were holding the castle. They commanded a small company of knights, archers, and peasant mercenaries. From atop the walls, the defenders of Nottingham defied Richard's threats and refused to open the gates.

Angered by their defiance, and not wishing to begin a long siege, Richard ordered his carpenters into action. They raised gallows at the base of the walls. Richard took several of John's men captive. He ordered them hanged at the end of ropes, in plain view of the castle battlements. The message to the men of Nottingham was: surrender the castle or die like criminals.

The plan worked. The lords of Nottingham Castle took one look at the bodies swinging from the gallows, and at the tall and kingly figure of Richard, and gave up their fight. Soon afterward, several other rebel strongholds surrendered to Richard's army.

Richard replaced the sheriffs and other officials loyal to John with his own men. A payment for the office was customary, even for men loyal to the king. In this way, Richard replaced the money paid to Henry as his ransom.

After putting down John's rebellion, Richard arranged another coronation. The ceremony took place on April 17, 1194. In front of lords, churchmen, and the members of the royal court, Hubert Walter, now the archbishop of Canterbury, placed the crown of England on Richard's head.

The ceremony was meant to assure the people of England that Richard had returned. He was no longer the prisoner or the vassal of the German emperor. He was again in control of the kingdom.

Richard would not stay long in England. The problems of the island kingdom did not interest him. It was not his concern if the people were poor and the treasury empty after the huge ransom paid for him. He was, first and foremost, the count of Poitou and the duke of Aquitaine. It was his land and his titles in southern France that he sought to protect.

FIGHTING IN FRANCE

Richard's purpose in restoring the English treasury was to pay for a campaign in France. He sailed from Portsmouth back to the continent in May. He rode to the town of Lisieux, where he met with his brother John.

Richard offered his forgiveness to his brother for the revolt in England. He also restored several estates in

England to John. He would not, however, allow John to command any fortified castles.

He might have forgiven John, but Richard would not forgive Philip. He blamed the king of France for all the trouble that had come about since the end of the Crusade. Richard rode from one town and estate to the next, chasing the French army but never bringing it to battle. He hired bands of mercenaries to ravage those places loyal to Philip.

In July, at the town of Freteval, Richard captured Philip's baggage train. In the king's chests he found royal charters. These documents gave people legal title to land and other property, by authority of the king.

Philip had granted these charters to landowners in Normandy, the territory of the Angevins. As a condition of their property, these Norman lords had to swear loyalty to the king of France. The charters made Richard realize that many Angevin lords had no loyalty to him.

The two kings finally met at the town of Tillieres, where they signed a truce. But Richard had no intention of keeping the peace. He hired a skilled mercenary captain, Mercadier, to assist him in the war against Philip.

For the next two years, Richard and Mercadier led their knights, archers, and infantry from Normandy to Aquitaine to Berry, in central France. On several occasions, they came close to capturing the French king. The two kings negotiated more truces. As Richard's forces conquered more territory, Philip gradually surrendered the lands he had claimed for France.

By the Peace of Gaillon in 1196, Philip surrendered every town he had wrested from Richard except Gisors and the territory around it known as the Norman Vexin.

THE CHATEAU GAILLARD

Not far from Gisors, now a French stronghold, Richard prepared for the reconquest of the Vexin. He ordered the building of a new fortress on the north bank of the Seine River. His masons and carpenters raised the Chateau Gaillard atop an imposing hill high above the river.

Richard designed the castle himself, giving the fortress elliptical walls. The walls allowed a free range of fire from every battlement. Richard spent nearly twelve thousand English pounds to build the castle, which took two years to finish.[1] The castle was so well constructed, and so difficult to besiege, that it has survived nearly intact to the present day.

In September 1198, Richard and Mercadier caught up with the French king on a road near Gisors. Philip was traveling with several hundred French knights, but at the sight of the Lionheart, he ordered a retreat.

Nearing the safety of Gisors, the knights rumbled across a flimsy bridge over the River Epte. Under the weight of the warhorses, men, and their heavy equipment, the bridge collapsed. Philip tumbled into the river in sight of Richard. The king laughed heartily at his drowning rival.

Richard charged the king's company and captured a hundred of Philip's knights. The French king was pulled from the Epte, coughing and choking, and fled the field in humiliation. Richard had scored yet another victory, one of the easiest of his career. Gisors was again in his hands.

DEATH AT CHALUS

In the early spring of 1199, Richard again took to the field. He rode south to the Limousin region. He had heard important news. He gathered a company and rode to the castle of Chalus.

This was the last chapter of Richard's life. Many legends grew up about the siege of Chalus. One legend claimed a treasure had been found at the castle. As the ruler in this region, Richard claimed the treasure. But the lord of Chalus defied Richard's claim. With a tiny force, he would defend his treasure and his castle.

Richard prepared for a siege of Chalus. He ordered his men into place. They fired arrows at the battlements. Behind the strong walls, only two knights, armed with crossbows, defended the castle.

The defenders walked the battlements. They aimed return fire down at Richard's troops. Richard scouted from the back of his horse. He had been to the Holy Land and back and fought in many savage battles. He didn't worry about his own safety. He did not even wear his heavy chain-mail shirt.

One of the defenders, a knight named Pierre-Basile, spotted the king riding at the base of the walls. The knight took careful aim and fired his bolt.

Traveling at great speed, the bolt struck Richard in the shoulder. The sharp point penetrated his clothes. The bolt pierced and tore his flesh.

Richard rode back to his tent. He pulled the bolt from his body. But the wound was infected. There were no medicines to cure the infection. Over the next few days, Richard grew sick and weak.

In the meantime, his men captured the castle of Chalus. They found Pierre-Basile and brought the man before Richard I died.

Pierre-Basille, the man who mortally wounded Richard, is brought before the king, who is on his death bed. The king pardoned Pierre-Basille. However, he was still executed after Richard I died.

Richard knew the nature of war. Every man fought as best he could. The duty of a soldier was to kill enemy soldiers and follow orders. By firing his bolt, and wounding the enemy king, the knight had been doing his duty. Richard forgave the man. But his followers were not so forgiving. They held Pierre-Basile prisoner.

Richard knew he was on his deathbed. He made his final instructions to his men. He wanted his body buried all over his realm. His followers were to bury his heart at the Norman capital of Rouen. His other organs would be laid to rest at Chalus. He wanted the rest of him brought to the abbey of Fontrevault, where his father, Henry, had been buried. On April 6, 1199, Richard I died.

In the meantime, Pierre-Basile was still held a prisoner. Mercadier, Richard's mercenary captain, felt deep anger at the knight for killing Richard. He ordered his men to flay the knight alive. Mercadier's men whipped the knight cruelly, then hanged him from a gallows.

THE FALL OF THE ANGEVIN EMPIRE

Richard had died without an heir. His brother John inherited the throne of England. The people of the Angevin realm in France did not support John. They accepted Arthur of Brittany as their overlord. Arthur was the son of Geoffrey of Brittany and the nephew of Richard I.

Under King John's rule, the Angevin empire disappeared. King Philip of France invaded Angevin territory in Normandy and Anjou. After 1214, the French king added Normandy, Brittany, Maine, Anjou, and the Touraine to the kingdom of France.

Aquitaine remained a possession of the English kings for another two centuries. In the early fourteenth century, England and France went to war over the rights and privileges of their kings. The war dragged on for over a century. At the end of this Hundred Years War, in 1453, France took permanent control of Aquitaine.

Richard I would go down in history as a great warrior, but a bad king. He neglected England while he reigned, and spent very little time there. He took more interest in fighting his crusade in the Holy Land than watching over his Angevin realm.

But Richard's exploits on the battlefield earned him fame throughout Europe, and in the Middle East. Richard inspired new generations of Christian warriors to crusade in the Holy Land. In the long history of the Crusades, only one man could match his ability to lead men into battle: his sworn enemy, the Muslim general Saladin.

The people of Europe revered Richard for his military prowess. But Richard's crusades left the English treasury empty. Because he was away for so long, the English landowners claimed more independence from the king. His brother John's harsh rule of England inspired a revolt among the English barons. These nobles demanded privileges of their own in the Magna Carta. This document, signed in 1215, made the king's will subject to the law.

In the Holy Land, Richard proved to be a skilled diplomat and general. He captured Acre and rebuilt the

The tomb of Richard I is at Fontevraud Abbey near Chinon, in Anjou, France.

crusading army after the disaster at Hattin in 1187. Realizing that he could not capture and hold Jerusalem, he arranged with Saladin to allow pilgrims to visit the holy city freely.

Richard also left much of the coast of Palestine under Christian control. He rebuilt and fortified the port cities of Tyre, Acre, Askalon, and Jaffa. He also left Cyprus under the control of the Lusignan family. The island served the crusaders as an important base for their campaigns in Palestine.

Richard would become a hero among poets, troubadours, and chroniclers. His brave exploits in Palestine were praised, while his destructive civil wars in France were forgotten. It was as a crusader, and not as a king, that the people of England and Europe would remember Richard Lionheart.

Chronology

1095—In France, Pope Urban II calls for a crusade. He asks Christians to fight Muslims for control of Jerusalem and the holy land of Palestine.

1154—Henry Plantagenet overcomes his strongest opponent, Stephen of Blois, and becomes Henry II, the new king of England. His Angevin realm stretches from the north of England to the Pyrenees Mountains.

1157—Richard is born on September 8, to Henry II and his queen, Eleanor of Aquitaine, at the palace of Beaumont in Oxford, England.

1168—Henry II makes an agreement with Louis, the king of France. The agreement recognizes Richard as the future lord of Aquitaine, a duchy of southwestern France, and engages Richard to marry Alais, the daughter of Louis.

1172—A formal ceremony endows Richard as the lord of Aquitaine.

1173—Richard joins his brothers and several lords of Aquitaine in a rebellion against Henry.

1174—The Treaty of Montlouis ends the war between Henry II and his rebellious sons. Henry imprisons his queen, Eleanor of Aquitaine.

1176—Richard fights opponents of Henry II in Aquitaine. He captures Limoges and Angouleme and captures Count William of Angouleme and Viscount Aimar of Limoges.

1179—Richard besieges and captures the powerful castle of Taillebourg, ending resistance to the Angevin rulers in Aquitaine. Later that year, the fifteen-year-old Philip becomes the new king of France.

1182—Henry encourages his sons Henry (the Young King) and Geoffrey to make war on Richard.

1183—Henry the Young King goes on a rampage in southern France, then dies from an attack of dysentery. Richard becomes heir to the throne of England.

1184—Geoffrey and John, the brothers of Richard, lead an army of mercenaries into Poitou and Aquitaine. Richard counterattacks in Brittany, Geoffrey's realm.

1185—Henry plays Richard off against his mother, Eleanor of Aquitaine. Richard agrees to surrender Poitou and Aquitaine to Eleanor.

1186—At Henry's urging, Richard battles the Count of Toulouse.

1187—A Muslim army under the Kurdish general Saladin defeats a Christian army at the Battle of Hattin, near the Sea of Galilee in Palestine. The Muslims capture Jerusalem. Calls for a new crusade arrive in Europe.

1188—Henry and Philip of France reach a truce at Gisors, on the border between Normandy and France. They vow to go on crusade in Palestine.

1189—Henry II is defeated by his sons and surrenders to Philip of France. Soon afterward he dies at the castle of Chinon. Richard is crowned the new king of England.

1190—Richard marches to Sicily in preparation for his crusade. He meets Philip at Messina and his troops battle the Sicilians. He makes a truce with Tancred, the king of Sicily.

1191—Richard sails from Sicily to Cyprus. His fiancee, Berengaria, and his mother reach Cyprus and contend with Isaac Comnenus, the island's governor. On May 12, Richard marries Berengaria. He then defeats the armies of Comnenus and sails to the port of Acre. The fortress of Acre surrenders after a short siege. Richard leads his armies south and battles the Muslims at Arsouf. He stops his army at Ramleh and turns back from a siege of Jerusalem.

1192—Richard fortifies the coastal city of Ascalon. In the summer, he marches east to Jerusalem. He retreats once again and relieves the fortress of Jaffa during a siege by Saladin. He agrees to a truce with Saladin, which allows Christians to visit Jerusalem and keeps some coastal ports in Christian hands. He sails back to Europe and, in disguise, begins to cross the continent on foot. Leopold of Austria orders his arrest and imprisonment in the castle of Dürnstein.

1193—Leopold turns Richard over to Henry VI, of the Holy Roman Empire. Henry negotiates Richard's release for a large ransom, to be paid from the treasury of England.

1194—Henry VI releases Richard, who returns to England. He puts down a rebellion inspired by his brother John. He returns to the continent and battles the armies of King Philip. He signs a truce with Philip at Tillieres.

1195—Richard and his mercenary captain, Mercadier, fight Philip's knights and armies in France.

1196—Richard and Philip sign the Peace of Gaillon. Philip surrenders towns he captured, except for Gisors.

1197—Richard makes plans for a stronghold overlooking the Seine River, known as the Chateau Gaillard. It will allow him to protect Normandy and carry out raids on the territory of the king of France.

1199—Fighting with a rebellious noble in the Limousin region, Richard besieges the castle of Chalus. A crossbow bolt strikes him in the shoulder. He dies from the infected wound on April 6. His brother John succeeds him as the king of England.

CHAPTER NOTES

INTRODUCTION

1. Philip Henderson, *Richard Coeur de Lion: A Biography* (London: Robert Hale Limited, 1958), p. 114.

2. Ibid., p 114.

3. James A. Brundage, *Richard Lion Heart* (New York: Charles Scribner's Sons, 1974), p. 117.

CHAPTER 1. THE ANGEVIN REALM

1. Harold Lamb, *The Crusades* (New York: Doubleday & Company, Inc., 1930), p. 7.

2. Amy Kelly, *Eleanor of Aquitaine and the Four Kings* (Cambridge, Mass.: Harvard University Press, 1950), p. 94.

3. Ibid., pp. 94–95.

4. Ibid., p. 60.

5. James Brundage, *Richard Lion Heart* (New York: Charles Scribner's Sons, 1974), p. 10.

6. Geoffrey Regan, *Lionhearts: Saladin, Richard I, and the Era of the Third Crusade* (New York: Walker, 1999), p. 6.

CHAPTER 2. THE SIEGE OF TAILLEBOURG

1. Amy Kelly, *Eleanor of Aquitaine and the Four Kings* (Cambridge, Mass.: Harvard University Press, 1950), pp. 192–193.

2. Muhammad J. Akbar, *The Shade of Swords: Jihad and the Conflict Between Islam and Chrisianity.* London: Routledge, 2002, p. 79.

CHAPTER 3. REBELLIONS IN THE ANGEVIN REALM

1. Amy Kelly, *Eleanor of Aquitaine and the Four Kings* (Cambridge, Mass: Harvard University Press, 1950), p. 216.

CHAPTER 4. HEIR TO THE ANGEVIN THRONE

1. Alison Weir, *Eleanor of Aquitaine: A Life* (New York: Ballantine Books, 1999), p. 245; James Brundage, *Richard Lion Heart* (New York: Charles Scribner's Sons, 1974), p. 56.

2. Ibid., p. 246.

3. Ibid., p. 247.

CHAPTER 5. THE KING OF ENGLAND

1. Alison Weir, *Eleanor of Aquitaine: A Life* (New York: Ballantine Books, 1999), p. 249.

2. John Gillingham, *Richard the Lionheart* (New York: Times Books, 1978), p. 132.

3. David Boyle, *The Troubadour's Song: The Capture and Ransom of Richard the Lionheart* (New York: Walker and Company, 2005), p. 68.

4. Ibid., p. 69.

5. Roger of Hoveden, "The Persecution of the Jews," *The Medieval Sourcebook*, n.d., <http://www.fordham.edu/halsall/source/hoveden1189b.html> (June 3, 2006).

6. Boyle, p. 67.

7. Gillingham, p. 149.

8. Ibid., p. 163.

9. Tim Boatswain, *A Traveller's History of Cyprus* (Northampton, Mass.: Interlink Books, 2005), p. 66.

Chapter 6. In the Holy Land

1. Geoffrey Regan, *Lionhearts: Saladin, Richard I, and the Era of the Third Crusade* (New York: Walker, 1999), p. 184.

2. Jonathan Riley-Smith, ed., *The Oxford Illustrated History of the Crusades* (New York: Oxford University Press, 1995), p. 236.

Chapter 7. The March to Jerusalem

1. Geoffrey Regan, *Lionhearts: Saladin, Richard I, and the Era of the Third Crusade.* (New York: Walker, 1999), p. 177.

2. Sir Steven Runciman, *A History of the Crusades, Vol. III: The Kingdom of Acre* (Cambridge, England: Cambridge University Press, 1954), p. 61.

3. Regan, pp. 209–210.

CHAPTER 8. RETREAT FROM THE HOLY LAND

1. David Boyle, *The Troubadour's Song: The Capture and Ransom of Richard the Lionheart* (New York: Walker and Company, 2005), pp. 152–155.

2. Amy Kelly, *Eleanor of Aquitaine and the Four Kings* (Cambridge, Mass.: Harvard University Press, 1950), p. 301.

3. Boyle, p. 196.

4. John Gillingham, *Richard the Lionheart* (New York: Times Books, 1978), p. 228.

5. D.D.R. Owen, *Eleanor of Aquitaine: Queen and Legend* (Oxford, England: Blackwell Publishers, 1995), p. 86; Boyle, p. 183.

6. Ibid., p. 87.

7. M.T. Clanchy, *England and Its Rulers, 1066–1272* (Malden, Mass.: Blackwell, 1998), p. 95.

8. Gillingham, p. 236.

9. Ibid., p. 237.

CHAPTER 9. THE LAST CAMPAIGNS
IN FRANCE

1. John Gillingham, *Richard the Lionheart* (New York: Times Books, 1978), p. 264.

GLOSSARY

battlement—The top of a castle wall. The battlement helped to conceal defenders. It allowed them to fire more easily against anyone laying siege to a castle stronghold.

bezant—A gold coin first minted during the late Roman Empire. Bezants were used until the twelfth century throughout Europe.

charter—A document giving its holder the right to titles, land, or money from income-producing goods or property. Kings granted royal charters in exchange for service to the crown.

courtier—A member of a medieval court, who serves a lord or king as adviser, entertainer, companion, clerk, or as the overseer of servants and defenders.

crossbow—A medieval weapon that fired an iron bolt at high speeds. Crossbows held a short bow mounted on a heavy wooden stock. They were fired with a trigger rather than pulled back and released by a soldier's hands. Crossbows could penetrate armor, both leather and iron. Crossbowmen firing a volley could devastate a line of infantry or knights. They were typically kept behind the front lines for their own protection, as they could not defend themselves in hand-to-hand combat.

domain—The property of a feudal lord, including the houses, fields, orchards, castles, villagers, and goods belonging to that property.

homage—A feudal ceremony, in which one man becomes the vassal of another. By tradition, during the ceremony of homage, the vassal placed his hands between those of his lord, while swearing to obey and serve his lord and fight when called upon.

knight—A skilled warrior on horseback, who fights at the bidding of his feudal lord. Knights inherited their titles and privileges. By the eleventh century, they held title to property granted by their lords in return for their services. They were equipped with the strongest armor and best weapons in the medieval army. They were mobile and could fight independently of archers and other foot soldiers.

mangonels—Catapults that could hurl heavy stones at high speed against the walls of cities or castles.

mark—A silver coin in use throughout northern Europe during the Middle Ages. England did not mint mark coins. Instead, they used a "mark" in written records as a unit of value, worth two-thirds of a pound.

mercenary—A man who fights solely for pay, without special loyalty to the state or lord he fights for.

tithe—A payment of money to a lord or king from their vassals or citizens of a town. The tithe could be based on income, property, or the produce of the land. It was often levied as a contribution to the church, as in the Saladin Tithe, which helped to pay for Richard I's crusade.

tournament—A medieval contest of strength and fighting skill. During a tournament, teams of knights on horseback battled with swords and lances. In single combats, two knights rode full tilt at each other, trying to throw the other to the ground with their weapons.

FURTHER READING

Crompton, Samuel Willard. *The Third Crusade: Richard the Lionhearted vs. Saladin.* Philadelphia: Chelsea House, 2004.

Doherty, Katherine M. *King Richard the Lionhearted and the Crusades in World History.* Berkeley Heights, N.J.: Enslow, 2002.

Hancock, Lee. *Saladin and the Kingdom of Jerusalem: The Muslims Recapture the Holy Land in A.D. 1187.* New York: Rosen Publishing Group, 2004.

Hilliam, David. *Richard the Lionheart and the Third Crusade: The English King Confronts Saladin, AD 1191.* New York: Rosen Publishing Group, 2004.

Hopkins, Andrea. *Damsels Not in Distress: The True Story of Women in Medieval Times.* New York: Rosen Publishing Group, 2004.

Madden, Thomas F. *Crusades: The Illustrated History.* Ann Arbor, Mich.: University of Michigan Press, 2005.

Nicolle, David, and Krista Smith. *The Third Crusade 1191: Richard the Lionheart, Saladin, and the Battle for Jerusalem.* Botley, Oxford, UK: Osprey Publishing, 2005.

Internet Addresses

Britannia.com: Richard I Coeur de Lion
<http://www.britannia.com/history/monarchs/mon27.html>

King Richard the Lionheart
<http://www.historic-uk.com/HistoryUK/England-History/RichardTheLionHeart.htm>

Life in a Medieval Castle
<http://www.castlewales.com/life.html>

INDEX